NATIONS OF THE WORLD

ITALY

Picot Cassidy

www.raintreepublishers.co.uk
Visit our website to find out more information about Raintree books.

To order:
 Phone 44 (0) 1865 888113
 Send a fax to 44 (0) 1865 314091
Visit the Raintree bookshop at www.raintreepublishers.co.uk to browse our catalogue and order online.

First published in Great Britain by Raintree, Halley Court, Jordan Hill, Oxford, OX2 8EJ, part of Harcourt Education Ltd.
Raintree is a registered trademark of Harcourt Education Ltd.

Produced for Raintree by the Brown Reference Group plc
Project Editor: Peter Jones
Designer: Joan Curtis, Seth Grimbly
Cartographer: William Le Bihan
Picture Researcher: Lizzie Clachan
Indexer: Kay Ollerenshaw

Raintree Publishers
Editors: Isabel Thomas and
    Kate Buckingham

Printed and bound in Singapore.

ISBN 1 844 21475 3 (hardback)
07 06 05 04 03
10 9 8 7 6 5 4 3 2 1

ISBN 1 844 21489 3 (paperback)
07 06 05 04 03
10 9 8 7 6 5 4 3 2 1

British Library Cataloguing-in-Publication Data

Cassidy, Picot
    Italy – (Nations of the world)
    1. Human geography – Italy – Juvenile literature
    2. Italy – Geography – Juvenile literature
    I. Title
    919.5

A full catalogue is available for this book from the British Library.

Front cover: Italian carabiniere
Title page: Ponte Vecchio, Florence

The acknowledgements on page 128 form part of this copyright page.

Every effort has been made to contact copyright holders of any material reproduced in this book. Any omissions will be rectified in subsequent printings if notice is given to the publishers.

Contents

Foreword

S ince ancient times, people have gathered together in communities
where they could share and trade resources and strive to build a
safe and happy environment. Gradually, as populations grew and
societies became more complex, communities expanded to become
nations – groups of people who felt sufficiently bound by a common
heritage to work together for a shared future.

Land has usually played an important role in defining a nation. People
have a natural affection for the landscape in which they grew up. They
are proud of its natural beauties – the mountains, rivers and forests –
and of the towns and cities that flourish there. People are proud, too,
of their nation's history – the shared struggles and achievements that
have shaped the way they live today.

Religion, culture, race and lifestyle, too, have sometimes played a
role in fostering a nation's identity. Often, though, a nation includes
people of different races, beliefs and customs. Many may have come
from distant countries. Nations have rarely been fixed, unchanging
things, either territorially or racially. Throughout history, borders have
changed, often under the pressure of war, and people have migrated
across the globe in search of a new life or because they are fleeing from
oppression or disaster. The world's nations are still changing today:
some nations are breaking up and new nations are forming.

The Italian people have one of the richest cultures in the world. It is
composed of many regional traditions that were previously part of
independent states. The earliest of these were the Etruscan and Roman
cultures that developed in central Italy, the latter the centre of a vast
civilization. Rome then achieved importance at the head of the Catholic
Church, and it was in the small **city-states** of the peninsula that the great
flowering of art that was the **Renaissance** began. Although only formed
into one nation in 1861, today Italy is a vibrant mix of its many parts,
combining its historical dominance in the arts with contemporary
excellence in design, fashion, agriculture and fine food and wines.

Introduction

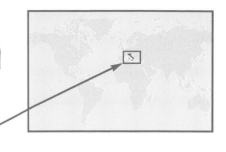

Many things come to mind when we think of Italy – tasty pizza and ice cream, elegant fashions and fast cars, romantic operas and fine art, to name just a few. Visitors to the country, though, remember Italy less for these individual things than for a general atmosphere – its beautiful old cities set amid lush countryside, its friendly, lively people and, above all, its warm and sunny climate.

Italy has a central position in southern Europe. It covers an area of 301,268 square kilometres (116,293 square miles). Mainland Italy consists of a long, narrow peninsula, shaped roughly like a leg, which sticks out into the Mediterranean Sea. There are also two large islands – Sicily and Sardinia – as well as other smaller islands. The largest island, Sicily, sits like a football on the 'toe' of Italy. To the west of the mainland, at about 'shin level', is the country's second-largest island, Sardinia. Italy's northern land borders are with France, Switzerland, Austria and Slovenia. The country's southernmost point is the tiny island of Lampedusa, which lies closer to the north African country of Tunisia than to Italy.

Although the nation of Italy was only unified in 1861 (see pages 66–8), the area now occupied by the country has had a profound effect on the history of Europe and the world. Italy once stood at the centre of the Roman

Filippo Brunelleschi's dome of Florence Cathedral – perhaps the greatest symbol of the Renaissance in architecture – dominates the city's skyline.

FACT FILE

- Italy became one country only in 1861. Foreign rule was ended in 1870.

- Between 1860 and 1973, 26 million Italians emigrated to other countries, especially to North and South America.

- Inside Italian territory are two independent republics – San Marino and the Vatican City.

- San Marino, which lies in the east of the Italian peninsula, is the oldest republic in the world. It was founded in the 4th century AD. It covers only 62 sq km (24 sq miles) and has only 24,000 inhabitants.

The French emperor Napoleon Bonaparte made the tricolore the flag of the Italian areas he conquered in 1796, changing the blue of the French flag to green because it was his favourite colour.

empire, and 2000 years ago, the ancestors of the Italian people had one of the most sophisticated and productive civilizations of the ancient world. With the rise of Christianity, the city of Rome became the centre of the **Catholic Church**, itself a major political as well as spiritual power. Later, in the 14th and 15th centuries, Italy became the centre of the artistic cultural rebirth of Europe known as the **Renaissance**, which developed in the small **city-states** of Italy, such as Florence and Pisa.

Today, Italy is a major player in the **European Union** (EU). It has the sixth-largest economy in the world and is a leader in agriculture, vehicle manufacture, fashion and design. The country's historic artefacts make it a magnet for tourists. In addition, Italy enjoys very varied terrain, from the snowy peaks of the Alps to the sun-drenched beaches of the south and the rich farming land of the central regions.

The flag of Italy has three vertical bands in green, white and red. Italians sometimes call their flag the *tricolore* because it has three colours. It was modelled on the French flag, which is blue, white and red. It became the official flag when Italy was united in 1861.

Before the euro was adopted, the Italian currency used to be the lira. One lira was not worth very much, so most prices were in thousands of lire.

In 2002, Italy – along with eleven other EU countries – adopted the EU's single currency, the euro, as its national currency. Until then, Italy's currency was called the **lira** (the plural is lire). Euro banknotes are the same throughout the EU, but the coins have one common side and one national side. Italy's euro coins feature images of important Italian people and places. The 2 euro coin, for example, shows a portrait by the Italian Renaissance artist Raphael (see page 97) of the Italian poet Dante Alighieri (see page 101).

The official language of Italy is Italian. It is a Romance language, which means that it comes originally from Latin, the language spoken by the ancient Romans. Italian is also an official language in the Ticino, the part of southern Switzerland that borders Italy. Before people spoke standard Italian – which is based on the dialect of Florence – people living in different areas of the Italian peninsula spoke their own dialects. Some of these dialects can be quite close to Italian, but they have some very different words. On the island of Sardinia, people speak Sard. At the beginning

The area around Bolzano is important as the centre of the Ladin language. Descended from Latin and once the mother tongue of the entire Tyrol, it now has only a few thousand speakers.

The national anthem

The Italian national anthem, *'Fratelli d'Italia'* ('Brothers and Sisters of Italy'), was written before Italy became reunited as a country. It was officially adopted as the national anthem in 1948.

The words are by Goffredo Mameli (1827–49), who died fighting for a united Italy. He wrote the words two years before his death. His friend Michele Novaro set the words to music. Mameli's song became very popular as a way of showing support for a united Italy, even though people could be arrested for singing it.

First verse

Brothers and sisters of Italy,
Italy has arisen,
With Scipio's helmet
Binding her head.
Where is Victory?

Let her bow down,
For God has made her
The slave of Rome.

Chorus

Let us gather in legions,
Ready to die!
Italy has called!

Second verse

We for centuries
Have been downtrodden and derided
Because we are not a people,
Because we are divided.
Let one flag, one hope
Bring us together;
The hour has struck
For us to join forces.
Let us gather in legions,
Ready to die!
Italy has called!

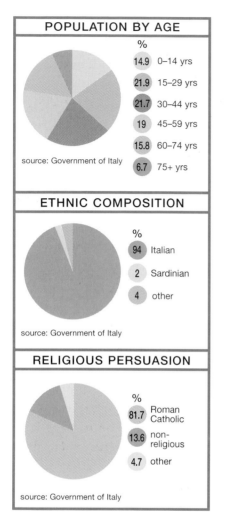

POPULATION BY AGE

%

14.9	0–14 yrs
21.9	15–29 yrs
21.7	30–44 yrs
19	45–59 yrs
15.8	60–74 yrs
6.7	75+ yrs

source: Government of Italy

ETHNIC COMPOSITION

%

94	Italian
2	Sardinian
4	other

source: Government of Italy

RELIGIOUS PERSUASION

%

81.7	Roman Catholic
13.6	non-religious
4.7	other

source: Government of Italy

Italy has a remarkably uniform population, which is largely Catholic. Compared to other major European nations such as the United Kingdom and France, there has been relatively little recent immigration.

of the 20th century, only 2 per cent of Italians spoke exclusively Italian; the rest used local dialects for day-to-day speech. Today, young people can often understand the local dialect but they tend to speak it less than their grandparents or their parents do.

Other languages are also spoken in Italy. People living in border areas often speak the languages of the nearby countries. In the Aosta Valley near France, around 100,000 people speak French. The north-eastern region of Trentino-Alto Adige near Austria has around 200,000 German speakers. In the same region, Ladin and Friulian are spoken by people of the southern Tyrol. Like Italian, these languages derive from Latin. Further east around Trieste, some people speak Slovenian. In the south of Italy, there are communities of Greeks and Albanians who settled in Italy in the 14th and 15th centuries and still speak Greek and Albanian.

Religion

Most Italians are Roman Catholics, but there are also **Protestant** minorities in the far north-east of the country. Altogether, Protestant groups number around 200,000 worshippers. The Jewish community has 35,000 members. There are also about 300,000 Muslims, mostly immigrants from Morocco, Tunisia and Senegal, who tend to live in the south or the industrial cities of the north.

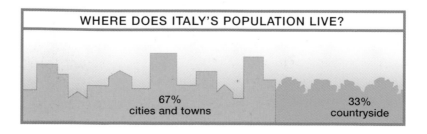

WHERE DOES ITALY'S POPULATION LIVE?

67% cities and towns

33% countryside

POPULATION DENSITY

Italy's population is largely clustered around its major cities, the industrial centres of Milan, Turin and Genoa in the north and the two regional capitals of Rome and Naples in the centre and south. During the industrial boom of the 1960s, large numbers of people from the agricultural south abandoned their poor farming lands in favour of the industrial suburbs of the north. Since the 1980s, the government has launched policies to encourage investment and population movement towards the south of the country.

PERSONS

Per sq km		Per sq mile
5		13
25		65
50		130
200		520

Despite a rapid increase in the immediate post-war period, Italy's population has now levelled off and will soon go into decline.

National symbols

The national emblem of Italy was chosen in 1946, when Italy became a **republic**. It is a five-pointed white star superimposed on a cogwheel. Around the left side of the cogwheel are laurel leaves and to the right are oak leaves. The star represents unity; the cogwheel, industry; and the leaves, republicanism. The national flower is the carnation. In addition to the national symbols, many of the major towns also have historic emblems. Venice has the winged lion; Florence, the lily; Rome, the she-wolf suckling its cubs. These symbols reflect the history of these cities as independent states.

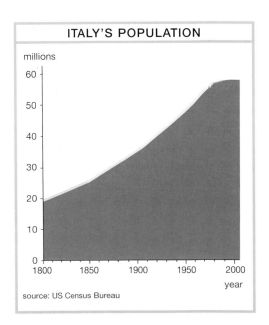

ITALY'S POPULATION

millions

source: US Census Bureau

Land and cities

'For wheresoe'er I turn my ravished eyes/Gay gilded scenes and shining prospects rise./Poetic fields encompass me around./And still I seem to walk on classic ground.'

From *A Letter from Italy* by 17th-century English writer Joseph Addison

The nation of Italy is surrounded on three sides by the Mediterranean Sea. The country is largely mountainous – low-lying areas comprise just 22 per cent of the country. Nevertheless, there is a great variety of landscapes, including snow-capped peaks in the north, lush green hills in the centre and rocky coastal areas, especially in the south.

From north to south, the country stretches 1200 kilometres (745 miles). From west to east, however, it varies between only 54 kilometres (87 miles) and 170 kilometres (105 miles) wide. The land borders to the north are 1932 kilometres (1198 miles) long. This is short in comparison to the coastline, which stretches for 7600 kilometres (4723 miles). This figure includes the coastlines of the 3766 islands that lie around Italy's mainland peninsula.

Italy lies in an earthquake zone, an area where the plates that make up the Earth's crust sometimes push against each other. Beneath the plates is magma, a molten rock that can rise up to the surface as an eruption through a volcano. Central and southern Italy have more earthquakes and volcanoes than the north.

To a large extent, the geographical differences between the northern **Alpine** region of Italy and the warmer southern region reflect differences between the Germanic culture of northern Europe and the more mixed Mediterranean culture of the south.

The composition of the Italian landscape, such as this area in Tuscany, has been an inspiration to artists for hundreds of years.

FACT FILE

- Italy is 78% hills or mountains, with many ranges over 702 m (2300 ft).

- The highest mountain in Italy is in the Monte Rosa massif (a large mountainous area) on the Italian–Swiss border. Its tallest summit, the Dufourspitze, is 4634 m (15,203 ft) high.

- Four seas wash the Italian coastline, all of which are part of the Mediterranean. The Ligurian Sea is off the west coast near Genoa, and the Adriatic Sea lies off the east coast. Between the mainland and the island of Sardinia is the Tyrrhenian Sea. The Ionian Sea lies east of Sicily.

ITALY'S TERRAIN

Plains
Less than 25 per cent of Italy is made up of plains and more than half of these lie in the Po Valley, the country's main agricultural region. In addition, there are smaller lands down the Tuscan coast and around the cities of Naples and Rome on the west coast, largely areas of reclaimed swamp land. In the southern region of Puglia are ancient plains levelled by the sea.

Uplands
Italy has two major mountain ranges, the Alps to the north of the country and the Apennines, which run down the centre of the peninsula. In addition, the country has a variety of upland landscapes, such as the sub-Apennines and the Abruzzi Mountains.

Coastal plains
The coastal areas of eastern Italy are largely fertile plains and there are more plains around the instep of Italy's 'heel'.

THE TERRAIN

Geographers divide Italy's terrain into eight land areas: the Alps, the Po Valley, the Adriatic Plain, the Apennines, Puglia (Apulia) and the south-eastern plains, the western uplands and the islands of Sicily and Sardinia.

The Alps

The Alps, the highest mountain range in Europe, curve across the top of Italy. They form the country's frontiers with its neighbours – France, Switzerland, Austria and Slovenia. Just over the French border is Mont Blanc, the highest mountain in Europe at 4807 metres (15,771 feet). The peaks of these ancient mountains are rocky and snow-capped all year. There are more than 1000 glaciers, which are remnants of the last Ice Age.

~ITALY~

FRANCE
GERMANY
AUSTRIA
SWITZERLAND
HUNGARY
SLOVENIA
CROATIA
BOSNIA HERZEGOVINA

Dolomites
Bolzano
Tyrol
Marmolada
Mountains
Adige R.
Dufourspitze
Udine
Trento
Belluno
Lake Como
Como
Treviso
Alps
Lake Maggiore
Varese
Verona
Trieste
Mt Blanc
Novara
Milan
Brescia
Venice
Padua
Pavia
Mantua
Gulf of Venice
Turin
Alessandria
Parma
Po River
Asti
Reggio
Ferrara
Cuneo
Modena
Savona
Genoa
Bologna
Ravenna
La Spezia
Massa
Forli
Rimini
Viareggio
Lucca
Florence
SAN MARINO
Pisa
Arno R.
Pesaro
Ligurian Sea
Livorno
Arezzo
Urbino
Piombino
Siena
Lake Trasimeno
Perugia
Ancona
Macerata
Elba
Assisi
CORSICA
Porto Santo Stefano
Terni
Adriatic Sea
Civitavecchia
L'Aquila
Pescara
Rome
Gran Sasso
VATICAN
Avezzano
Latina
Abruzzi Mountains
Manfredonia
San Severo
Campobasso
Mt Vesuvius
Benevento
Bari
Naples
Salerno
Potenza
Castellana Caves
Brindisi
Taranto
Lecce
Sassari
Gulf of Taranto
Otranto
Nuoro
SARDINIA
Rossano
Oristano
Punta La Marmora
Cosenza
Campidano
Tyrrhenian Sea
Cagliari
Catanzaro
Ionian Sea
Stromboli
Aeolian Islands
Messina Strait
Trapani
Palermo
Messina
Reggio di Calabria
SICILY
Mt Etna
Taormina
Marsala
Catania
Gela
Siracusa
Ragusa

KEY

cities and towns by population

◇ over 1,000,000

▣ 200,000 to 1,000,000

◯ 50,000 to 200,000

● under 50,000

other symbols

▲ high points

-- country border

| 0 | 50 | 100 | 200 km |
| 0 | 30 | 60 | 120 miles |

N

The Dolomites, which stretch across the northern region of Trentino-Alto Adige into the Veneto, are popular with walkers. The area contains many refuges (publicly maintained cabins) with a few provisions, where walkers can take shelter from the weather.

Lower down the mountains, there are forests of beech, oak and chestnut, as well as conifer. Road and railway tunnels have been dug through the rock to allow traffic and trains to reach other countries, even in winter weather.

At the north-eastern end of the Alps, the mountains are formed of limestone rocks called 'dolomites', which give the massif its name, the Dolomites. The highest point in the Dolomites is the Marmolada, which rises to 3342 metres (10,964 feet). The limestone has been eroded to make a landscape of steep, jagged rocks shaped like towers and domes. These contrast with the lower slopes, which curve gently and are covered with green pastures, pine trees and crops.

The Po Valley and the Adriatic Plain

Italy's longest river is the Po. It rises in the Alps near the border with France and runs east to the Adriatic Sea. The river flows for 652 kilometres (405 miles) through a flat plain called the Po Valley. Sometimes the Po floods, although a system of dykes helps to control flooding. Italy's second-longest river, the Adige, flows 410 kilometres (255 miles) through the Po Valley. It rises in the Dolomites and flows to a delta south of Venice.

The city of Turin is the capital of the wealthy Piedmont region. It is also home to the Fiat car company.

More than 60 per cent of all the lowland in Italy is in the Po Valley. Made up of the river's rich silt, this area has the best farmland in Italy. The area is the most densely populated part of the country, with two large cities, Milan and Turin. Industrial zones and suburbs lie around the cities.

The Adriatic Plain is a small plain to the east of the city of Venice. The eastern half – the Carso Plateau – borders on Slovenia. The land here is very poor.

The Apennines

The Apennines, a major range of mountains, extend nearly the whole length of Italy, making a long zigzag about 1000 kilometres (620 miles) down the peninsula. In the north at Genoa, the Apennines first follow the west coast, then reach across to the east coast at Pesaro. Further south, the Apennines veer westwards again towards the Mediterranean and continue from Naples down to the Messina Strait.

The Apennines are 193 kilometres (120 miles) at their widest point in central Italy. The only Apennine glacier, Calderone, in the rugged Gran Sasso area, is the southernmost glacier in Europe.

The massif of the Gran Sasso (whose name means literally 'large rock') contains the highest of the Apennine peaks. These tower over the regions of Abruzzo, Le Marche and eastern Lazio.

17

The southern end of the Apennines is a volcanic area. The most famous volcano is Mount Vesuvius – 1185 metres (3891 feet) high – near Naples. Gases often force their way up through the craters. There have been devastating eruptions in the past and there could be others at any time. Sometimes glowing lava flows out of the volcanoes, destroying buildings and crops.

Western uplands and plains

This area stretches along the Tyrrhenian Sea from just south of Genoa in the north-west right down to Rome and past Naples along the central western coast. It is densely populated, especially around the great urban centres of Rome and Naples.

The land here is very fertile, second only to the Po Valley for its quantity of agricultural produce. In the north, grain crops are grown and cattle are raised. The land here is excellent for fruit and vegetable farming. There are also many vineyards in the region. As land for agriculture is precious, marshland was drained during the 1930s in the Maremma of southern Tuscany and also in Agro Pontino in Lazio.

In central Italy, the Arno River – 241 kilometres (150 miles) long – rises in the Apennines and flows west. It passes through the cities of Florence and Pisa before reaching the Ligurian Sea. The Tiber, at 405 kilometres (252 miles) Italy's third-longest river – flows through the capital, Rome. In 1966, many rivers in central Italy burst their banks and there was widespread flooding. Florence was submerged as the waters of the Arno rose. Buildings and artworks were damaged, some beyond repair. In the city, signs on walls show high water marks (see page 31).

The Tuscan countryside is characterized by rolling hills covered in vineyards. The Tuscan region is Italy's most important wine producer, notably for the wines of the Chianti, the area that lies between Florence and Siena.

Puglia and the south-eastern plains

Most of Puglia, down in the 'heel' of Italy, comprises a series of flat, limestone plateaux, with some higher ground in the Gargano Peninsula. The largest plain area is the Tavoliere Plain. The Castellana Caves are a series of limestone caves, with spectacular stalactities and stalagmites.

Sicily and Sardinia

The largest island in the Mediterranean, Sicily covers 25,709 square kilometres (10,027 square miles). It is a triangle shape, and in ancient times, was called *Trinakria*, the Greek word for 'triangle'. The highest point is Mount Etna, an active volcano that rises to 3340 metres (10,959 feet). An earthquake destroyed Messina on the north of the island in 1908, and in 1968 another earthquake caused damage to the west of the island. Etna's last major eruption was in 2002, when lava damaged more than 100 homes in Santa Venerina.

Mount Etna looms over the Sicilian coast south of Taormina. It is Europe's biggest volcano and one of the largest in the world.

Sardinia, the second-largest Mediterranean island, covers 24,089 square kilometres (9300 square miles) and is largely mountainous. About 1.6 million people live on the island. Because of the remoteness of the interior, the people here have remained relatively distinct and are known throughout Italy for their black hair and distinctive looks. The island has two mountain ranges separated by the long plain of Campidano, which cuts a diagonal south-east across the island. Just south of the centre of the island is the Gennargentu Range. The highest point, at 1834 metres (6017 feet), is the Punta La Marmora.

THE REGIONS OF ITALY

Italy is divided into twenty regions, which are then further subdivided into a number of provinces. Each of the regions has a strong local character and usually its own dialect. The map shows the twenty regions, which are listed on the left with their capitals. These regional capitals are indicated with a dot on the map.

ABRUZZO L'Aquila
BASILICATA Potenza
CALABRIA Catanzaro
CAMPANIA Naples
EMILIA-ROMAGNA Bologna
FRIULI-VENEZIA GIULIA
Trieste
LAZIO Rome
LIGURIA Genoa
LOMBARDY Milan
LE MARCHE Ancona
MOLISE Campobasso
PIEDMONT Turin
PUGLIA Bari
SARDINIA Cagliari
SICILY Palermo
TRENTINO-ALTO ADIGE
Trento
TUSCANY Florence
UMBRIA Perugia
VALLE D'AOSTA Aosta
VENETO Venice

The region of Piedmont, whose name comes from the French for 'foot of the mountain', was a French-speaking region until the end of the 19th century. Although it was ruled by France for many years, it played a leading role in the unification of Italy.

THE REGIONS

Italy is divided into twenty administrative regions, each with its own regional capital. The largest region is the southern island of Sicily; the smallest is Valle d'Aosta (Aosta Valley) in the north-west. Many of the regional boundaries are based on the historic areas into which Italy was divided before 1861.

There are still differences between the regions, not just in landscape and climate but also in food, customs, language and lifestyles. People in Italy are very attached to the place that they come from. Even when they move away, they still feel that their birthplace or region is very important.

Five of the regions – Sicily, Sardinia, Valle d'Aosta, Trentino-Alto Adige and Friuli-Venezia Giulia – have a special status because they are islands or because they border other countries. Valle d'Aosta is near France, while Trentino-Alto Adige and Friuli-Venezia Giulia border Austria and Slovenia, respectively.

At regional level, voters elect a regional council. In turn, the members of the regional council elect an executive and its president as the regional government. Each region is subdivided into provinces. There are 94 provinces in total. In turn, a province is divided into *comuni*. A *comune* could be a village, a small town or a city. There are 8091 *comuni* in Italy. Each *comune* has an elected mayor and a council. They look after local matters such as public transportation, rubbish collection and street lighting.

The Alpine village of Dolonne sits right on the border with France in the shadow of Mont Blanc.

The north

The north is traditionally the wealthiest part of Italy and is home to much of the country's industry and most fertile land. In the north-west corner are four regions: Valle d'Aosta, Piedmont, Liguria and Lombardy. Valle d'Aosta is Italy's smallest region. The highest Alpine peaks lie within the region, and many mountain towns serve as ski resorts, attracting thousands of tourists in winter.

Lying partly in the Alps but mostly in the Po Valley, Piedmont is Italy's second-largest region. The Po River flows through the capital, Turin. Turin is a bustling manufacturing centre and home of the Italian car industry. South-east of Turin, in the Monferrato Hills, famous

The small coastal town of Manorola in Liguria is one of the Cinque Terre, five fishing ports based around cliffs that plunge into the sea. People here produce wines on steep vineyards, some of which are accessible only by boat.

wines are made around Asti. Near Alba in the south of Piedmont, trained dogs hunt for aromatic white truffles from the soil.

Liguria occupies a small strip of territory where the Alps plunge into the sea. The regional capital is the ancient city of Genoa. The sunny Ligurian coast, with its elegant resorts and picturesque fishing villages, attracts many visitors. To the east of Piedmont is the wealthy region of Lombardy. This sprawling region is Italy's centre for industry, banking and fashion. To the north, Lakes Maggiore and Como are popular destinations for summer trips out of the regional capital, Milan.

The north-east corner of Italy has three regions: Trentino-Alto Adige, Friuli-Venezia Giulia and the Veneto. The Veneto stretches from Lake Garda east to the regional capital, Venice. Like many other northern regions, Veneto is a wealthy area with a thriving industrial sector, much of it centred around Venice's industrial suburb of Mestre. There are many old towns and cities in the Veneto, including Verona and Padua. Out in the countryside are handsome villas, once the homes of the powerful and wealthy, who liked to spend their summers away from the sweltering heat of the busy cities.

North of Veneto is Trentino-Alto Adige, which stretches north into the Dolomites. The region has two capitals, Trento and Bolzano, one for the Italian-speaking majority and one for the German-speaking minority. The regional assembly sits in each capital alternately. Many towns here have a German name and an Italian one. Bolzano's German name, for example, is Bolzen.

The region of Friuli-Venezia Giulia borders Slovenia and has a Slovenian-speaking minority. The capital, on the eastern edge of the region, is the sea port of Trieste.

Italians top a dish of pasta or risotto with finely grated Parmesan cheese. Real Parmesan cheese comes from the Emilia-Romagna region, especially around the city of Parma.

Lovelorn in Verona

Romeo and Juliet, or Giulietta e Romeo as the Italians say, have made the city of Verona famous around the world. The couple were never real people but come from the English dramatist William Shakespeare's reworking of a 15th-century story. Many visitors still come in search of the lovers. An old house in the city centre is called Juliet's House, and people stand there and imagine the famous balcony scene in which Juliet calls for her lover. Some people write

graffiti on the walls.

Those who cannot visit Verona sometimes write letters to the city about their romantic problems. Most of the letters come from France, Italy, China, Poland and the USA. A team of paid staff and volunteers takes turns answering the letters in a variety of languages, signing them 'Juliet' or 'Juliet's secretary'. A psychologist advises on the more complicated situations. Each year, there is even a prize for the best letter.

Central Italy

The centre of Italy comprises seven regions: Emilia-Romagna, Tuscany, Umbria, Le Marche, Lazio, Abruzzo and Molise. The geographical centre of the Italian peninsula is at Rieti in Lazio.

Emilia-Romagna is the northernmost of the central Italian regions. It is a region of fertile plains famous for its agricultural products, including wheat, maize and sugar beet, as well as dairy products. It takes part of its name from the Via Emilia, an ancient Roman road that crossed the Po Plain south-east from Piacenza to Rimini on the coast. The regional capital is Bologna, famous for its arcaded streets, its large university and its rich, tasty cuisine. Bologna is also an industrial centre with steel, engineering and food-processing plants.

Tuscany shares a long regional border with Emilia-Romagna. Its capital is the beautiful historic city of Florence. Tuscany and its southern neighbour, Umbria, have landscapes of rounded green hills. In addition to Florence, the region has many historic towns, including Siena, Pisa, Arezzo and Lucca, which attract visitors from all over the world. The land along the Arno River

Politically, central Italy was the base of support for the Communist Party. The wealthy region of Emilia-Romagna is now controlled by the PDS, the reformed version of the Communist Party.

Bologna is famous for its medieval towers, which were originally built as lookouts. Wealthy landowners later tried to outdo each other with the height of the buildings.

is fertile, producing wheat and maize, as well as olives and grapes for wine. Prato, near Florence, is one of the main centres for textile production in the country.

Off the coast of Tuscany is the Tuscan Archipelago. The largest island in this group is Elba. Largely mountainous, the island depends on tourism and iron-ore mining, which has taken place there since ancient times.

The region of Umbria south of Tuscany is landlocked. It is famous for its old hilltop towns, including Assisi, Gubbio and Spoleto. The capital, Perugia, also sits high on a hill and was home to an ancient people known as the Etruscans (see pages 48–9), who once rivalled the Romans. The town of Assisi also attracts millions of visitors every year. Saint Francis, who founded the religious order of Franciscan monks, was born in Assisi in 1182 and spent his life there. In 1998, its beautiful old basilica was badly damaged in an earthquake and priceless frescoes (wall paintings) were lost.

The hilly, secluded region of Le Marche (the Marches) lies on the eastern side of the Apennines. The regional capital, Ancona, is an ancient sea port.

The capital of Italy, Rome, lies in the Lazio region. On hot summer weekends, Romans head west to the beach at Ostia, which was a port in ancient Roman times. Today, the only modern port along Lazio's long, sandy coastline is at Civitavecchia. To the south of Rome are the Alban Hills, where the pope has his summer home at Castel Gandolfo. Close to the sea and separated from it by low sandy hills are the Pontine Marshes. For a long time, this was an area of unhealthy swamps, but in the 20th century much of the area was drained and new towns were built.

Abruzzo and Molise are both mountainous, remote regions on the eastern side of the Apennines. Until 1963,

At the lake

Not far from Perugia is Lake Trasimeno. It is the largest lake in south and central Italy, covering 128 sq km (50 sq miles). It is well known for a fierce battle fought on its northern shores in 217 BC. Hannibal of Carthage and his army defeated the Romans, killing 16,000 soldiers. Today, visitors come to the lake for more peaceful pursuits. The waters of the lake are only 7 m (23 ft) deep and therefore remain relatively warm.

The region of Lazio is also known as Latium. This region was traditionally ruled by the great families of Rome, and in its countryside many of their magnificent villas can still be seen.

Molise was part of Abruzzo. The landscape of Abruzzo is wild, with rugged mountains. L'Aquila, the capital, is an old medieval town. Abruzzo is often called the 'Park Region' because 30 per cent of its land is protected by environmental laws. The highest Apennine peak is in the Abruzzo – the Gran Corno, at 2914 metres (9560 feet).

The south

The south of Italy is also known as the **Mezzogiorno**, which means 'midday' as well as 'south', evoking images of its dazzling, sun-drenched landscapes. Traditionally, the south has been one of the poorest areas of Italy, with little industry and poor farmland. The area also has a reputation for lawlessness and is the homeland of the **mafia**, a criminal fraternity (see page 74). The four regions of Campania, Puglia, Basilicata and Calabria are very beautiful, famous for their high, craggy mountains, fragrant lemon orchards and deep-blue coastal waters.

The capital of Campania is Naples, the largest city and home to the main industrial zone in the south. Curving along the Bay of Naples, the region includes the

Capital of the Campania region, Naples is a loud, chaotic, bustling city with a successful textiles industry and a thriving black market. The city is home to over 1 million people.

Under the volcano

The looming outline of Mount Vesuvius and its plumes of smoke are a familiar sight to the people of Naples. It might seem strange that people would want to live so close to an active volcano. The main reason why people first founded villages near Vesuvius is the richness of the soil. Over time, as lava solidifies and breaks down, it becomes very fertile soil.

People grow a great range of crops in the rich, black soil that surrounds the lower slopes of the crater. There are orange and lemon groves and vineyards. Lacryma Christi (literally, 'tears of Christ'), a famous white wine, is produced from grapes grown near Vesuvius. The wine label shows a picture of the volcano.

Volcanologists – scientists who study volcanoes – believe that Vesuvius could be due for another major eruption like that which destroyed the city of Pompeii. They monitor the behaviour of the volcano carefully, trying to detect signs of any impending eruption.

ancient Roman town of Pompeii. When the volcano Vesuvius erupted in AD 79, Pompeii was covered by rocks and ash. The virtually intact city was only redis-covered and excavated centuries later. Splendid villas and gardens were uncovered, together with brightly coloured frescoes and other art treasures. The petrified bodies of the city's inhabitants were found lying just where they died, often curled up on the ground as they sought to protect themselves from the burning ash and poisonous fumes. Today, the Campania coast is famous as a luxury holiday destination and is dotted with scenic resorts, such as those along the Amalfi coast and the towns of Positano and Sorrento.

On the Adriatic coast, the region of Puglia forms the 'heel' of Italy. The capital is the port city of Bari, which is the second-largest city of the south. It is a thriving centre of new technology industries and hosts an impor-tant trade fair every September. Basilicata, between Puglia and Campania, has a short coastline on the Tyrrhenian Sea and another, longer one on the Ionian Sea. Some of the land is poor because trees have been cut

Carlo Levi, a famous Italian author who was exiled to a remote region of Basilicata by the Nazis, described his experiences in *Christ Stopped at Eboli*. Published in 1945, it described the bleak nature of life in southern Italy at the time.

down and valuable soils have been lost through erosion. Potenza, the capital, is in the centre of the region.

In Matera, there are stone houses built around caves in the ravines that cut across the town. Calabria is the mountainous 'toe' of Italy, which pokes out between the Tyrrhenian and the Ionian seas. It has more fertile land than Basilicata and a few towns with a little industry, including Catanzaro, the regional capital. Just north of the tip of Calabria is Aspromonte, a rugged massif. From the top, there are views across the Messina Strait to Sicily.

Greek temples

Just outside the Sicilian town of Agrigento stands a group of Greek temples unique outside of Greece itself. The town was founded in 581 BC by Greek colonists. The temples were built mostly in the 5th century BC, though the oldest, the Temple of Hercules, was begun at the end of the 6th century BC. The most complete is the Temple of Concorde with its sacrificial altar, which survives largely intact because the temple was converted into a church in the 6th century AD.

Sicily

Sicily has a complex history. Waves of different people – Phoenicians, Greeks, Romans, Arabs, Normans and Spanish – have occupied it and settled there over the centuries. These peoples left behind a rich variety of monuments, including temples, mosques, churches, castles and palaces.

The population of Sicily is 5.1 million. The capital is the ancient city of Palermo in the west, but the business centre is on the east coast at Catania. An oil refinery in the east handles crude oil extracted offshore near Gela and Ragusa. There are also petrochemical plants nearby.

Many Sicilians still have a close connection with the land. Around 40 per cent of the population still work in agriculture. The main agricultural products are wheat, grown in the inland plains, and citrus fruits and grapes from the coastal zones.

The influence of the mafia (see page 74) in many parts of life, including business, is still very strong in Sicily. Many people want to take back power from organized crime and to get rid of corruption and improve everyone's standard of living. There is also a political movement, *La Rete*, which campaigns against the mafia.

Off the north coast of Sicily are the Aeolian, or Lipari, Islands. In ancient times, people thought of the islands as the home of the winds. This volcanic archipelago of seven islands includes the active volcano of Stromboli. Lava flows often erupt and drop dramatically from the side of the volcano into the sea. At night, the brilliant, fiery glow of the lava can be seen for kilometres.

Sardinia

Like Sicily, the island of Sardinia has been settled by many different people. Scattered across the island are thousands of conc-shaped houses, left by the first people, the Nuraghi, who came here in around 2000 BC.

For many years, Sardinia was relatively isolated, linked only to the Italian mainland by ferry. Perhaps for this reason, it managed to preserve its rich folk traditions, many of which date back hundreds of years. Every May, Sardinians dressed in traditional costumes take part in colourful processions.

The island's beautiful, rocky coastline now attracts many visitors. The first large-scale tourist development was the Costa Smeralda in the north of the island. Modern airports at Cagliari, Alghero and Sassari bring visitors in by air.

Fishing is a major industry in Sardinia and the local cuisine reflects it, with local dishes of grilled lobster, fish stews and bottarga, a type of caviar made from mullet eggs.

CLIMATE

Italy is in a temperate zone, which means that it is generally neither extremely hot nor cold. However, the further south you go, the hotter and drier the country becomes. The mountains and the sea also influence the climate. For example, the west coast is usually warmer and wetter than the east.

In the Alps, the highest mountain peaks are covered in snow all year round. The snow line starts at 3108 metres (10,200 feet) in Valle d'Aosta and as low as 2545 metres (8350 feet) on the eastern side of the Alps. The Alps form a barrier against the cold winter weather of northern Europe, so winters around Lakes Garda, Como and Maggiore are generally mild. In January, the nearby city of Milan has an average minimum temperature of 1 °C (35 °F), compared to 4 °C (39 °F) around Garda. The Ligurian Sea coast also has a mild winter because it is protected by the Alps and the Apennines. A little further south in the Po Valley area, however, winters are cold and frosty and summers are hot and humid. Rain falls mainly in spring and autumn. Snow sometimes falls in Lombardy and Emilia-Romagna.

Central and southern Italy have a Mediterranean climate. Summers are long, hot and dry. In Tuscany, they last three-and-a-half to four months; in Calabria,

Midsummer temperatures are fairly uniform throughout the Italian peninsula. In winter, the central region of the Po Valley and the areas around Italy's northern fringes frequently have temperatures below freezing, while in the south, they barely drop below 10 °C (50 °F).

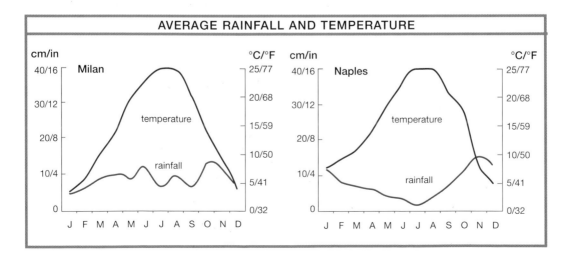

AVERAGE RAINFALL AND TEMPERATURE

Milan

Naples

Florence floods, 1966

The floods in Florence in November 1966 killed several people and caused huge amounts of damage to buildings and artworks. Here Professor Umberto Baldini, head of the Florence Restoration Board, describes his experience:

… I rushed over to the restoration centre but luckily there was no sign of any water there, so I went immediately on to the Uffizi; when I arrived I saw that the water had already nearly reached the height of a tram. The water was nearly a metre and a half [5 ft] deep in Piazza Duomo and the situation was already serious in Piazza della Signoria as well. I managed to get inside the Uffizi but the water was already up to my waist.

Inside the Uffizi we tried to remove as many paintings as we could to safety; these included works by Giotto, Tiepolo, Mantegna, as well as the Virgin *by Filippo Lippi. We also managed to lift the* Coronation of the Virgin *by Botticelli high enough to prevent the water from touching, because it was too big to go through the door.*

Once we had got the paintings to safety, we headed for the Vasari Corridor above the Ponte Vecchio to try to save the paintings that were in danger there. The bridge shuddered and we thought it was going to fall down. We managed to remove the paintings and immediately returned to the Uffizi from where we were able to see the fury of the Arno [River] from the upstairs windows. We could see that the Ponte Vecchio was likely to fall down at any minute. Then it was given a violent blow by a lorry that had been carried away by the terrifying floodwaters, which caused the walls to collapse like a pack of cards. This terrible impact made an enormous hole in the bridge but also created a path for the floodwaters. That blow was what saved the Ponte Vecchio.

It was 3:30 in the morning when the waters finally went down and the city was left in total darkness.

summer lasts five months and winters there are mild. Calabria and Sicily are surrounded by sea, so they have higher temperatures than the areas further north, together with low rainfall. The average minimum January temperature in Palermo in Sicily is 8 °C (44 °F). In July and August, the temperature rises to 30 °C (86 °F). Sardinia's climate is influenced somewhat by the Atlantic. It can also get the hot sirocco wind blowing up from Africa or the cold mistral wind from the north-west.

WILDLIFE AND VEGETATION

Italy's animals and plants are as varied as its landscapes. However, because large areas of Italy are farmed or settled, the country's most interesting wildlife lives in remote places such as mountains or coastal waters. In the Alps live species that are well adapted to the cold climate. The coats of stoats and Alpine rabbits as well as the feathers of mountain partridge turn white to act as camouflage in the winter snow, while other animals, such as the marmot, hibernate (sleep through the winter) to conserve their energy and keep warm.

In the Gran Paradiso National Park in the Alps, ibex are pro-

The chamois is one of the species that is protected in the Alps region. Italy's large hunting community is a real threat to wildlife, particularly in the north of the country.

tected and can roam freely. These mountain goats have large horns that curve backwards. In the central Alps, there are chamois, a type of goat antelope, with straight horns that point up and back. Alpine birds include black grouse and the rare golden eagle. Other mountain animals such as lynx, stoats, brown bears and wolves are now rare. Brown bears are protected and are more often found in the wilder parts of Abruzzo. Remote areas of Sardinia are home to fallow deer, mouflon sheep and wild boar.

In the seas off Italy, especially further south, are large numbers of white sharks, bluefin tuna and swordfish. In the warmer southern seas, there are also red coral and sponge, a marine animal with a fibrous skeleton.

Centuries ago, Italy was covered with forests. As towns and cities were built, many of these disappeared. The Umbra Forest in the Gargano Peninsula in Puglia is one of the last of these original forests in Italy, with beeches and oaks. There are also beechwoods in Calabria, as well as silver fir and pine forests in Abruzzo.

Where these ancient forests have disappeared in the Mediterranean parts of the Apennines, low scrub called *macchia* has grown up. *Macchia* includes wild olives, oleander, laurel, myrtle, holm oaks, cork oaks and cluster pines. This is now considered perhaps the most characteristic vegetation of mainland Italy. Cypresses and olive trees are a typical part of the landscape in sunny Mediterranean regions. Cork oaks have a thick layer under the bark, which is often used for making bottle corks and other cork products. In the mountain meadow lands of Calabria and Basilicata can be found vetch, bent grass and white asphodel. By contrast, the areas of the Po Valley contain almost nothing of the original forests because they have been converted into farmland.

The tall, slim forms of cypress trees are a characteristic of the Italian landscape, particularly in the central regions of Umbria and Tuscany.

Italy's national parks

To protect Italy's rare or endangered species of wildlife, trees and plants, there are nineteen national parks, with five more planned. Altogether, they will cover an area equivalent to 5% of Italy's land area. The two largest parks are in the Alps: Stelvio (1350 sq km; 521 sq miles) and Gran Paradiso (700 sq km; 270 sq miles). The smallest is on Cape Circeo, along the coast south of Rome. The areas protected are very varied, including part of the Alps, the volcano Vesuvius, coastal areas and even whole islands and archipelagos. There are also many regional parks throughout the country.

VALGRANDE
STELVIO
GRAN PARADISO
DOLOMITI BELLUNESI
M. FALTERONA-CAMPIGNA
FORÉSTE CASENTINESI
MONTI SIBILLINI
ARCHIPELAGO TOSCANO
GRAN SASSO
MAIELLA
GARGANO
ISOLA DELL'ASINARA
ABRUZZO
VESUVIO
CIRCEO
GOLFO DI OROSEI-MONTI DEL GENNARGENTU
CILENTO E VALLO DI DIANO
POLLINO
CALABRIA

Rural life

As with Italy's industry, farms in Italy are usually family concerns, a fact that is reflected in the small size of most holdings, although there are large farmlands in the Po Valley. Here, wheat and maize are the most common crops. In remoter regions, farming concentrates on wine-making and livestock farming. In the south, the larger farms are worked by people who live in nearby towns. In Sicily, the population is clustered around 'peasant cities' that reflect the historical structure of Sicilian society.

CITIES

Italy is unusual in not being dominated by any one city. Each region has its own capital and a strong sense of identity. This reflects the country's past, when areas such as Naples and Sicily, or **city-states**, such as Florence, Pisa and Venice, were separate states. In terms of population, the largest cities are Rome, Milan, Naples and Turin, all with populations over 1 million. In many respects, however, the smaller cities are equally important.

Rome

Rome is one of the world's great historical cities. It enjoyed two periods of importance. In ancient times, it was the centre of a civilization and a mighty empire that spread across Europe, west Asia and north Africa. Later, the city was the most important centre for Christianity and, as such, its power and influence are still felt across the globe. Because of its age-old importance, Rome is often referred to as the 'Eternal City'.

The city centre is a fascinating mixture of ancient monuments and bustling city life and noisy traffic. The original centre spreads over seven hills: the Palatine, Aventine, Capitoline, Quirinale, Viminale, Esquiline and Celian.

From the top of the Capitoline Hill the remains of the Forum can be seen (see page 46). This was the place where the people of ancient Rome came to worship, settle political issues, do business or simply socialize. On a walk through the grassy site a visitor can see what is left of temples and other public buildings. Other ancient monuments – triumphal arches, public baths, temples, villas – can also be seen in the city. Outside the centre are the catacombs, the underground tombs of the early Christians.

The Spanish Steps, which lead up to the church of Trinità dei Monti – seen here in the distance are one of the main tourist attractions of Rome. They run down to the Piazza di Spagna (Spanish Square), which took its name from the main building there, the Spanish Embassy.

The ancient city of Rome was built around the seven hills. The centre of the modern city is largely built on the right bank of the Tiber, with the Vatican on the left. To the south of the current city lie the remains of the Forum, the Colosseum and, further south, the remains of the giant baths complexes. The city's principal street is the narrow thoroughfare of the Via del Corso.

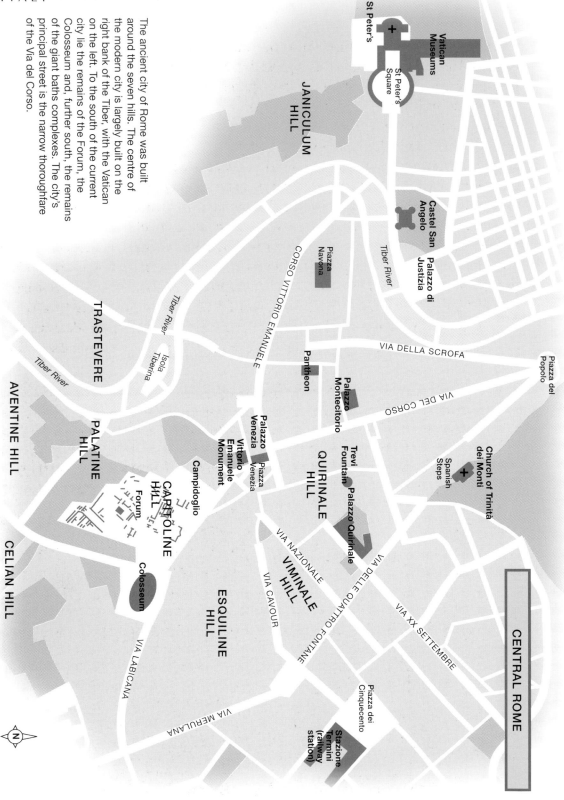

CENTRAL ROME

St Peter's

Vatican Museums

St Peter's Square

Castel San Angelo

Palazzo di Justizia

JANICULUM HILL

Tiber River

Piazza Navona

CORSO VITTORIO EMANUELE

VIA DELLA SCROFA

Piazza del Popolo

Pantheon

VIA DEL CORSO

Palazzo Montecitorio

TRASTEVERE

Tiber River

Isola Tiberina

Tiber River

Palazzo Venezia

Piazza Venezia

Vittorio Emanuele Monument

Trevi Fountain

Spanish Steps

Church of Trinità dei Monti

AVENTINE HILL

PALATINE HILL

Campidoglio

CAPITOLINE HILL

Forum

QUIRINALE HILL

Palazzo Quirinale

VIA DELLE QUATTRO FONTANE

VIA NAZIONALE

VIMINALE HILL

VIA XX SETTEMBRE

CELIAN HILL

Colosseum

ESQUILINE HILL

VIA CAVOUR

VIA LABICANA

VIA MERULANA

Piazza dei Cinquecento

Stazione Termini (railway station)

N

On top of the Capitoline Hill is the Campidoglio, an elegant **Renaissance** square designed by Michelangelo (see page 98) in 1536. Around the square are a 13th-century church and the Capitoline Museums, housing one of the great collections of Roman sculpture. At the foot of the Capitoline, in **Piazza** Venezia, stands the **Palazzo** Venezia, once the Venetian Embassy and later the centre of Mussolini's **fascist** government (see page 71).

From the Piazza Venezia, the Via del Corso, lined with fashionable shops and cafés, runs north to the Piazza del Popolo, one of the city's largest squares. The piazza was once a gateway to the city and the gate can still be seen. In the centre of the piazza is an ancient Egyptian obelisk.

The Piazza Navona, a pleasant square of 18th-century houses, has at its centre the Fountain of the Four Rivers, a **Baroque** structure by Gian Lorenzo Bernini

Rome's ornate Monument to Victor Emmanuel II was built in honour of Italy's first king after unification. The Romans call it 'the typewriter' because of its shape, but visiting Americans called it 'the wedding cake' because its white marble never discolours.

The Colosseum

The largest Roman buildings were great feats of engineering. The 1st-century Colosseum still stands near the Forum. This vast amphitheatre, which took twelve years to build, has a 527 m (1729 ft) circumference and stands 57 m (187 ft) high. Four levels of seating for 80,000 spectators were supported by a structure of vaults and arches hidden behind a simple, curving outside wall. A linen awning was stretched across the top to protect spectators from the sun and rain. The arena could be flooded for naval and aquatic displays. People went to watch gladiators fight each other or wild animals, and races and naval battles.

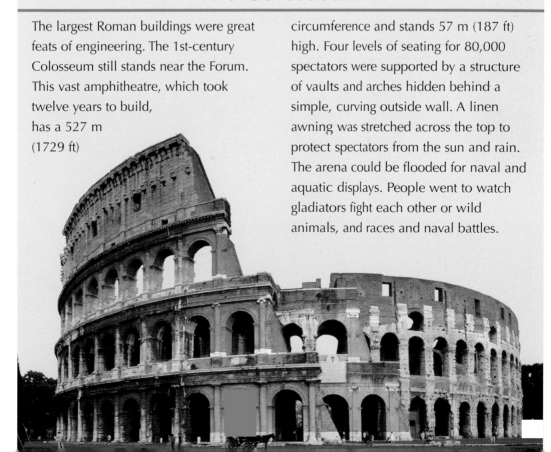

Rome underground

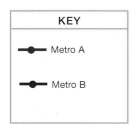

The Roman underground has two intersecting lines that meet at the main railway station, Termini.

(1598–1680). In the 18th century, the piazza would be flooded and Roman aristocrats would float around in horse-drawn boats. Another Baroque fountain is a famous landmark in Rome. The Trevi Fountain is an elaborate monument created by Nicol Salvi in 1762. It has a large sculpture of a sea god in a chariot drawn by two seahorses. There is a custom that, standing with your back to the fountain, you throw in two coins. The first coin is so that you will come back to Rome and the second is to have a wish granted.

On the opposite side of Via del Corso stands the Pantheon. Previously a Roman temple, in AD 609 it was consecrated as a church. The building is one of the masterpieces of Roman architecture. Its diameter, at 43 metres (164 feet), is exactly the same as its height – a perfect sphere would fit inside it, indicating the building's original role as a temple to the planetary gods. It is covered by a vast dome, supported only by the struts that run down through the concrete walls. Its dome was made possible by the use of concrete mixed with rubble, which created a solid mass that could be stretched over a large area, thus creating a vast interior uninterrupted by supports. The building was to have a major influence on European architecture, such as the domes of the Panthéon in Paris, St Peter's Basilica in Rome and St Paul's Cathedral in London.

When Romans go out for the evening, they may visit areas like Trastevere on the west bank of the Tiber, which has many restaurants and cafés, or Testaccio to the south, which is popular with young people and has lively discos and nightclubs. Central Rome is served by an extensive underground and light railway system, although new lines have been halted by the discovery of archaeological remains.

The Vatican

The Vatican City, from which the **Roman Catholic** Church is governed, occupies 44 hectares (109 acres) within the city of Rome. At Easter, up to 300,000 worshippers gather outside St Peter's to hear the pope give his blessing. As they gather in St Peter's Square, they are surrounded by the magnificent colonnade created by Gian Lorenzo Bernini between 1656 and 1667. Two semicircles, made up of four rows of colossal columns, curve in towards the façade of St Peter's Basilica. The basilica stands on the site where St Peter was allegedly buried after he was martyred. It was based on a plan conceived in the 15th century, but the actual building was mostly completed in the 16th and 17th centuries and involved some of the greatest architects of the Renaissance.

Inside the Vatican buildings are masterpieces painted by Raphael and Michelangelo. Michelangelo spent four years painting the ceiling of the Sistine Chapel, where cardinals meet to elect the pope. The chapel is named after Pope Sixtus IV and was completed in 1481.

In addition to the church itself, the Vatican also houses a series of museums containing some of the greatest treasures in the Western world, including Renaissance painting, classical sculpture and Etruscan, Greek and Egyptian artefacts. Also enclosed within the Vatican City is the Castel San Angelo, a vast castle built by the Roman emperor Hadrian as his mausoleum and later used by the popes as a fortress in times of siege.

Florence

Because they have so many historic buildings and price-less art treasures, the cities of Florence and Venice are among the most popular tourist places not just in Italy but in the world. Both cities depend to a large extent on tourism, but the people who live there often feel the pressure of the millions of visitors who come every year.

Florence stands on the Arno River. The most famous bridge over the river is the Ponte Vecchio (Old Bridge), a 14th-century structure lined with jewellery stores. Many of the buildings in the historic centre of Florence were constructed during the Renaissance. They often have plain, regular façades with overhanging roofs that give shelter to passers-by.

Walking north from the Arno, visitors pass the Uffizi Gallery, which the Florentine leader Cosimo the Great had built in the second half of the 16th century. It was originally an office building for work in the city government (its name means 'offices'), but now it houses the greatest collection of Italian Renaissance art in the world. The paintings are arranged chronologically. There are works by 13th-century painters such as Cimabue, Giotto and Simone Martini. The most famous exhibits are the works of Renaissance painters. Two paintings by Sandro Botticelli (1445–1510) are well known worldwide: his *Birth of Venus* and

Of Florence's six central bridges, the Ponte Vecchio was the only one not to be mined when the Nazis attacked the city in 1944. Adolf Hitler gave direct instructions that the historic bridge was not to be damaged.

Built in 1345, the Ponte Vecchio's upper story contains the Vasari Corridor, which links the Palazzo Vecchio with the Palazzo Pitti.

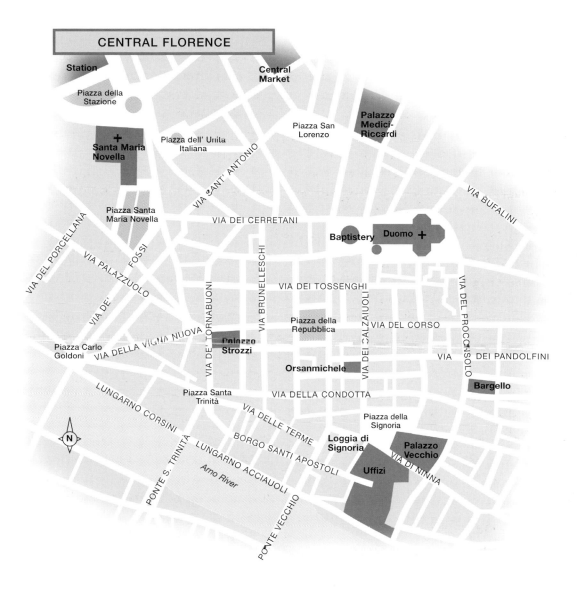

CENTRAL FLORENCE

Station

Central Market

Piazza della Stazione

Palazzo Medici-Riccardi

Piazza San Lorenzo

Piazza dell' Unità Italiana

Santa Maria Novella

VIA SANT' ANTONIO

VIA BUFALINI

Piazza Santa Maria Novella

VIA DEI CERRETANI

Baptistery   Duomo

VIA DEL PORCELLANA

VIA PALAZZUOLO

FOSSI

VIA BRUNELLESCHI

VIA DEI TOSSENGHI

VIA DE'

VIA DEI TORNABUONI

Piazza della Repubblica

VIA DEL SALZAIUOLI

VIA DEL CORSO

VIA DEL PROCONSOLO

Piazza Carlo Goldoni

VIA DELLA VIGNA NUOVA

Palazzo Strozzi

VIA   DEI PANDOLFINI

Orsanmichele

Bargello

Piazza Santa Trinità

VIA DELLA CONDOTTA

LUNGARNO CORSINI

VIA DELLE TERME

Piazza della Signoria

BORGO SANTI APOSTOLI

Loggia di Signoria

Palazzo Vecchio

N

PONTE S. TRINITA

LUNGARNO ACCIAUOLI

VIA DI NINNA

Uffizi

Arno River

PONTE VECCHIO

Primavera (Spring). In *Primavera* (see page 97), the figure of Lorenzo the Magnificent (1449–92) can be seen on the left, portrayed as the god Mercury with a bow and arrows. Lorenzo sponsored many artists. Works by Michelangelo, Raphael and many other great painters are also on view in the Uffizi.

Past the Uffizi Gallery is the Piazza della Signoria, the main square of historic Florence. So many statues are dotted around that it is like an outdoor sculpture exhibition. There are copies of famous statues such as

Florence is famous for its museums such as the Bargello (sculpture), the Uffizi (painting) and the palaces of its great families, such as the Medici and the Strozzi.

41

The tower of the Palazzo Vecchio, the ancient council building of Florence, is seen here from the roof of the cathedral. In the background is the fort of Belvedere.

Michelangelo's *David* (the original is in the city's Accademia museum) and Cellini's sculpture of the ancient Greek hero Perseus (the original is now in Florence's sculpture museum, the Bargello). The Palazzo Vecchio (or Old Palace, also known as the Palazzo della Signoria) on the square was the seat of the city government, the *signoria*.

Further along Via dei Calzaiuoli is the *duomo* (cathedral) of Santa Maria del Fiore. It was begun in 1296 but took almost 150 years to finish. The exterior is covered in designs of pink, white and green marble, topped by a soaring red-tiled dome. The dome was designed by Filippo Brunelleschi (1377–1446), who brought Renaissance ideas to architecture. There was no scaffolding suitable for building a domed roof over such a large building until Brunelleschi came up with the revolutionary idea of building up the dome in self-supporting horizontal layers that did not need so much scaffolding. Stone steps wind around the dome to the top to give a view over Florence.

Food is sold in a large, covered market, the *Mercato Centrale* (Central Market). The streets nearby are lined with open-air stalls selling clothes, leather goods and jewellery, all of which are important industries in Florence. Fashion and shoe shops are clustered along Via dei Calzaiuoli and Via de' Tornabuoni.

Venice

With a population of only 75,000 people, Venice has 23 million tourist visitors a year. They come out across the lagoon from the mainland by car, tour bus or train to see an extraordinary city. It was originally built up on stakes driven into mudbanks, which then formed the islands that we know today. The city has canals instead of roads and streets. Venetians do not go to work by car – they walk or take a *vaporetto* (waterbus). Two main bridges, the Rialto and the Accademia, cross the Grand Canal, which functions as Venice's long main street.

Large motorboats act as taxis. Large deliveries are made by water and smaller ones by hand cart. Rubbish is removed from the Grand Canal by small boats with a metal-gridded scoop at the front. Power lines and gas pipelines run underwater across the lagoon from the mainland. Police officers and firefighters use boats to get around and do their jobs. It is even possible to reach the airport, named after the Venetian explorer Marco Polo, by taking a boat.

The Canale Grande (Grand Canal) is Venice's main thoroughfare and curves through the city for 3 kilometres (2 miles).

Gondolas are traditional black Venetian boats. They are powered by a gondolier, who uses a long oar to push and steer the boat along. He stands at the back of the gondola and leans on his oar sticking out on the left of the boat.

The city came into being during the 5th and 6th centuries when people escaping from tribes invading from the north came from the nearby mainland and took refuge in the islands of the lagoon. The refugees built on the flat islands by sinking thousands and thousands of wooden piles to make foundations for their houses. To go from one island to another, they built bridges. As the city and its buildings grew, these separate islands became the city of Venice. It is built on 117 small islands, and has 400 bridges crossing its 150 canals.

The best way to gain a first impression of Venice is to take a *vaporetto* down the Grand Canal. It is about 3 kilometres (2 miles) long and twists in an S-shape through the city. On the way, it passes fine palaces built centuries ago. Their typical windows go up into a point, something like a **Gothic** arch. At the south end is the Piazza San Marco, Venice's main square. On three sides it has three-storey stone buildings with arcades at ground level. Small orchestras play in some of the street-level cafés.

On the fourth side of the square is the Basilica San Marco, the richly decorated **Byzantine** basilica dedicated to St Mark, Venice's patron saint. The symbol of the city is a winged lion that rests its paw on a book. Next to the basilica is the pink-and-white patterned **Doge's** Palace, built in the 14th century. From here the doge (ruler) of Venice and the **republic's** government controlled the city's affairs.

Water, water, everywhere

Every year from 1173 to 1797, the Venetians held a ceremony where they rowed out into the lagoon. The doge, the ruler of Venice, dropped a gold ring into the sea, saying 'We wed thee, sea, in token of our perpetual rule'.

The idea of the ceremony was to show the Venetians' power over the sea, but they are often reminded of the sea and its power. Sometimes when the tide is high, large puddles of water form across the Piazza San Marco. When a very high tide is expected, usually in winter, sirens are sounded three to four hours before. On every *vaporetto* (waterbus) station, there are maps showing safe routes when the tide is exceptionally high and floods parts of the city.

High tides are made worse by the fact that the city is sinking. For many years, engineers have discussed building a system of floodgates to protect Venice from the effect of high tides.

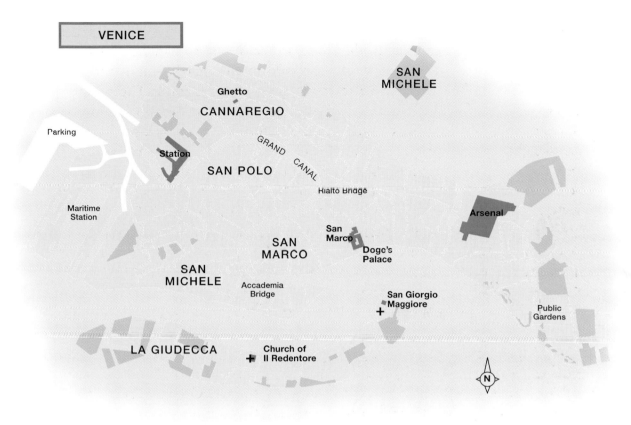

VENICE

There was a network of spies to report on activities that were considered against the interests of the Venetian republic. Enemies of the state were put in prison. The way through the palace to the prison goes over the Bridge of Sighs. The bridge is named because of the sighs made by prisoners as they crossed over. The other famous Venetian bridge is the Rialto, which crosses the Grand Canal and was a trading centre during the Renaissance.

Away from the broad Grand Canal, many of the streets are more like a maze of narrow alleyways that spread out from central squares. The city is divided into districts called *sestieri*. Every house in a *sestiere* is numbered, as well as being in a street. An address in the district of San Polo might be given as San Polo 1789, but to get there, you have to know that that house is on Calle Sturion. In the San Marco district, the house numbers go right up to 5562.

The main part of the Venetian islands is bisected by the Grand Canal. The historic centre of government used to lie around San Marco. The Arsenal, where Venice's impressive fleet was built, stood to the east.

Past and present

'Now we've made Italy, let's make Italians.'

19th-century Italian independence fighter Francesco Crispi

The land of Italy has been a meeting place of cultures for thousands of years. Its central position in the Mediterranean linked it with the trade routes of the ancient civilizations that developed in the region. Maritime trade with Phoenicia (near present-day Lebanon) and the states of ancient Greece brought profound cultural changes.

With the rise of Rome, however, the peninsula itself became the centre of the ancient world, controlling the largest and most powerful empire the world had ever seen. It was to the capital of this empire that the first Christians came, so that with the fall of Rome in AD 476, the city became the centre for the new religion. The spiritual and temporal power exerted by a succession of Italian popes in the following 1000 years stretched over most of Europe. The artistic flowering of the **Renaissance** was a product of flourishing mercantile **city-states**, such as Florence and Venice. Thereafter, Italy's history was one of gradual decline and foreign domination. It was only with the independence movement of the mid-19th century that the many separate states of the Italian peninsula were unified.

The last century of Italian history has been among its most turbulent. First there was the rise of **fascism** and, after World War Two, the threat of terrorism and corruption at the heart of the Italian state.

Many of the buildings in Rome's Forum were destroyed by fire in the 3rd century AD. Afterwards, many of the same stones were used to build churches.

FACT FILE

● The Roman empire was vast. It stretched from present-day Scotland south to the deserts of north Africa, and from the Caspian Sea west to the Atlantic Ocean.

● The 365-day year was introduced by Julius Caesar in 46 BC. In 1582, Pope Gregory XIII introduced a new calendar with leap years in years divisible by four and in century years that could be divided by 400. It is known as the Gregorian calendar.

● The Italian Christian Democrat Party was part of every Italian government from 1946 until its defeat in the elections of 1996.

EARLY PEOPLES

The spread of human occupation in Italy began early in comparison to northern Europe. Since 2000 BC, many different peoples have settled there. Around 1200 BC, the Ligurians and the Italics came down from the north. The Ligurians were Bronze Age settlers who moved down from what is now southern France and came to live in central Italy, near present-day Rome. The Italics came from near the Danube River in central Europe.

MAGNA GRAECIA AND ETRURIA

People from the eastern end of the Mediterranean explored the coast of Italy from about 5000 BC. The Phoenicians founded Carthage in north Africa and set up trading posts in Italy. By the 8th century BC, the Greeks began to found colonies in Sicily and southern Italy. Altogether, these colonies – including Syracuse, Agrigento, Crotone and Taranto – were called Magna Graecia (Greater Greece).

These Etruscan terracotta horses come from the Ara della Regina temple in Tarquinia near Rome. They date to the 3rd century BC.

Philosophers, scientists and writers came to live in the Greek colonies, and cities were built with large temples and open-air theatres. At Agrigento in Sicily (see page 28) and at Paestum near Naples, parts of the temples remain. While the Greeks were settling southern Italy and Sicily, in central Italy the Etruscans were founding cities. The Etruscans are still something of a mystery. No one is sure where they came from originally. At first, the Etruscans occupied the areas around the Arno and Tiber rivers and the Apennines. Later, they moved up into the Po Plain and down towards Rome. A federation of twelve city-states – including Volterra, Fiesole, Arezzo, Perugia and Chiusi – made up the region of central Italy that we know as Etruria.

The Etruscans became rich by mining iron, copper and silver and trading around the eastern Mediterranean area. Their cities were built on high ground and surrounded by defensive walls. They also built bridges, streets and canals and developed the use of the arch and barrel vault.

THE ROMAN REPUBLIC

The first Roman settlement was greatly influenced by its civilized Etruscan neighbours. At first, it was ruled by kings. Both the Etruscans and the Romans co-existed peacefully until the defeat of the Etruscans at Veii and the incorporation of the town into Roman territory in 396 BC. Over the next 100 years, the Romans took over the former Etruscan territory.

The founding of Rome is officially dated to 753 BC and from this time it was ruled by a line of seven kings. Early Rome was a regional centre largely administered by several powerful families. The **republic** was set up in 509 BC so that no single family could take power. The republic made the people of Rome the ultimate authority, although in reality power was concentrated in the hands of a few families. Every year, two consuls were elected; one looked after the army and the other was responsible for state administration.

There was also a **Senate**, which was a kind of assembly that discussed and approved laws. The senators came from the most important aristocratic families in Rome. Roman citizens usually wore a toga – a loose robe made of one piece of cloth wrapped round the body.

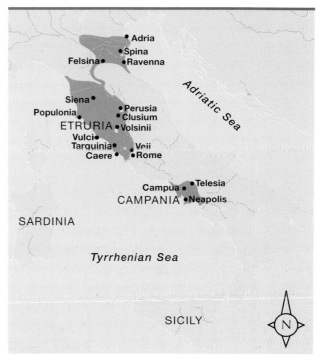

ETRURIA c.530 BC

The map shows the high point of Etruscan civilization in the 6th century BC. The names of many of today's Italian cities, such as Perugia (Perusia), Naples (Neapolis) and Ravenna, had Etruscan names.

Rome's conquest of Greece and of the former Greek terrritories in the 2nd and 1st centuries BC had a profound effect on the cultural life of the empire. The hitherto practical and rather coarse Roman republic was transformed into a centre of learning. Greek ideas flourished in the success of Roman civilization.

Consuls wore a special white toga with a purple border to show their status. The ordinary people were called plebeians and had no role in public affairs. Ten tribunes of the people represented them in government offices.

The Romans began to expand their territory, fighting and later forming alliances with the other tribes of Latium (the area around Rome). These were the Sabines, the Aequi and the Volsci.

Other tribes came to challenge the Romans. In 390 BC, the Gauls crossed the Alps and defeated the Roman army. Rome was almost destroyed and had to be rebuilt.

By 338 BC, the Romans had conquered their former allies, including the Etruscans. The Samnites, the last of these Italian peoples, were defeated in 290 BC.

In the eastern Mediterranean, the Greeks also began to worry that the Romans would become too powerful and want to take over Magna Graecia. In 280 BC, King Pyrrus landed an army of 25,000 men in southern Italy. They defeated the Romans in two battles, but the Greek army lost 8000 soldiers. A third battle was fought, in which more Greek soldiers were killed, and Pyrrus took his army back to Greece, leaving the Romans in control of the whole peninsula. A 'Pyrrhic victory' still means a victory that is won at too high a cost.

The Carthaginians, who had their capital at Carthage in north Africa and colonies in Sardinia and western Sicily, were worried that the Romans would take over their Mediterranean trade. Between 264 and 146 BC, the Romans defeated the Carthaginians in three wars, known as the Punic Wars.

Very civilized!

Life as a wealthy Roman was very comfortable. The Romans lived in large villas. The main rooms of the house opened off a central atrium (courtyard) with a pool in the centre. The floors were decorated with beautiful mosaics of trees, plants and scenes from legends or everyday life, and walls had bright frescoes (wall paintings). In winter, there was central heating under the floors. In the dining room, long couches were set around the table so Romans could lie down while eating. The hard housework was done by slaves, who had been sold into slavery by poor families or captured in war.

Gradually, more territories were added to Rome's empire. Hispania (the Iberian peninsula encompassing present-day Spain and Portugal) was ceded by the Carthaginians after the Second Punic War. By 146 BC, Greece was a province of Rome. Other areas around the shores of the eastern Mediterranean were also under Roman control. By 49 BC, the whole of Gallia (Gaul), including all of modern France, was part of the Roman empire and Rome controlled the Mediterranean.

As the Roman territories became larger, rivalry developed among ambitious generals who wanted to take control. With their armies, generals such as Sulla, Pompey and Julius Caesar made power bases in the provinces from which they threatened the central government in Rome. After a civil war in which he defeated his fellow consul Pompey, Julius Caesar became the dictator of Rome. Rome was no longer a republic. Although he was a clever ruler, Caesar's increasing arrogance annoyed the Romans. In 44 BC, he was assassinated at the Senate by those who wanted to restore the republic.

Little is left today of Carthage, in present-day Tunisia. It was once the centre of a great trading empire that rivalled that of the Romans in the Mediterranean.

THE EXPANSION OF THE ROMAN EMPIRE

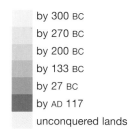

by 300 BC
by 270 BC
by 200 BC
by 133 BC
by 27 BC
by AD 117
unconquered lands

The greatest expansion of Roman power started in the 1st century BC.

THE FIRST EMPEROR

The ruler who followed Julius Caesar became Rome's first emperor. He was Caesar's great-nephew, Octavian, who took control after Caesar's death. He reorganized the administration of Rome. In 27 BC, he took the title of Augustus (which means 'sacred'). During his long reign of more than 40 years, Augustus Caesar brought stability to the Roman empire.

When Augustus Caesar died in AD 14, his son Tiberius became emperor. Tiberius was followed by Augustus' grandson, Caligula, in AD 37. Caligula ruled for only four years, until he was assassinated. He did many strange and cruel things during his reign. He had his wife, Drusilla, put to death, and had his horse appointed as a consul.

An international language

The language of the Romans was called Latin. It takes its name from Latium, the area around the city of Rome. Latin was used across the Roman empire. Later, the Catholic Church also used Latin as its official language. In the Middle Ages, between AD 476 and 1453, it was an international language used for official documents and by university students. It is still used in the naming of species.

You may think you do not know any Latin, but we use Latin words in English all the time. When you're talking about the time, you probably say a.m or p.m. to indicate whether you are talking about the morning or the afternoon. You are using Latin. The letters a.m. stand for *ante meridiem*, before midday, and p.m. for *post meridiem,* after midday. Now look up 'AD' and 'etc.' in a dictionary.

The next emperor was Claudius, Caligula's uncle. Claudius was an efficient ruler who added Britannia (Britain) to the empire in AD 42. After Claudius died in AD 54, his adopted son Nero became emperor.

In the years of Nero's reign as emperor, Rome was filled with stories of his cruelty. A large part of the city was damaged by fire in AD 64, and Nero blamed the Christians, followers of a new religion. He had them persecuted and tortured. He had both of his wives murdered. Finally the Roman Senate condemned Nero to death, but he committed suicide.

After Nero's death, there was confusion as to who should rule Rome. For the second half of the 1st century, a number of emperors brought stability and a better life for the people of Rome. In AD 69, a general called Vespasian took control and became an efficient emperor. Under Emperor Trajan's reign from 98 to 117, the Roman empire reached

Augustus Caesar, who ruled for 45 years, boasted that he found Rome a city of brick and left it a city of marble.

Diocletian made huge administrative changes in the empire and in the Roman army. In AD 303, one of his edicts began a decade of persecution against the Christians.

This Roman sarcophagus (stone coffin) of Livia Primitiva from the early 3rd century has the Christian symbols of the fish, good shepherd and anchor inscribed on it.

its greatest extent. Hadrian, who followed Trajan, reorganized Roman laws and had defensive forts built along the imperial borders.

In order to make administering such a vast empire easier, Emperor Diocletian (AD 245–313) divided it into eastern and western parts. The western capital was still in Rome, while the eastern capital was at Byzantium (present-day Istanbul in Turkey). Diocletian chose to rule from Byzantium.

A NEW RELIGION

Jesus Christ lived and died in a Roman province: Palestine. After his death, the new religion of Christianity became popular among people in the Roman empire, but it was forbidden. Christians could be persecuted, punished or even executed for their religion, so they worshipped secretly. Things changed when Constantine the Great became emperor.

There was trouble in the Roman empire because the eastern and western parts threatened to break apart.

Before a battle in AD 313, Constantine's army looked very weak compared to the enemy forces. Legend has it that Constantine saw a cross glowing in the midday sky with some words written in Greek, meaning 'In this sign, conquer'. He made a promise that, if he won the battle, he would allow Christians to worship freely. Just before his death in AD 337, Constantine was baptized a Christian. Christianity later became the official religion of the Roman empire.

In the second half of the 5th century, the Barbarian tribes formed distinct political units. Their cohesion threatened Rome and the city finally fell in AD 476.

After Constantine died, there were more and more invasions from tribes living on the northern borders of the empire. Many of them were being attacked themselves as the Huns, led by Attila, pushed across from central Asia. The Anglo-Saxons invaded the province of Britannia. The Burgundians occupied the area between the Rhine and the Rhône rivers, while the Franks gradually took over western Gallia.

By AD 410, a Visigoth army, led by Alaric, captured Rome. Later they left the Italian peninsula and settled in the region of southern France and Spain. The end of the Roman empire came in AD 476 when Odoacer, a Barbarian leader, deposed the emperor Romulus Augustulus from the throne. It was the end of the Roman empire in the west, although the Romans continued to rule the eastern part of the empire from Byzantium.

BARBARIAN INVASIONS IN THE 5TH CENTURY

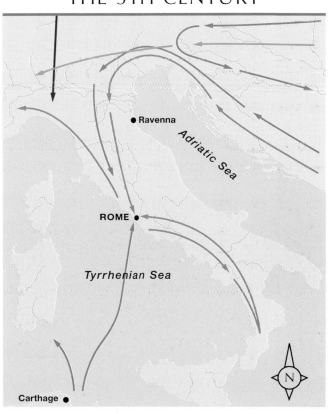

Ravenna

Adriatic Sea

ROME

Tyrrhenian Sea

Carthage

N

→ Huns
→ Ostrogoths
→ Visigoths
→ Vandals
→ Lombards

CHARLEMAGNE

After the fall of the Roman empire, different people struggled for control of the Italian peninsula. The only areas with some order were on the east coast from Ravenna down to Ancona, Puglia and Calabria, which remained under the control of the eastern emperor at Byzantium. Rome was governed by the pope.

Around AD 560, a Germanic tribe called the Lombards invaded Italy. There were not many of them, but they took advantage of the confusion to push down the peninsula, destroying towns as they went.

The Lombards converted to Christianity, made laws and began to rebuild towns and cities and encourage trade and agriculture. The daughters of the Lombard

*This map shows
the extent of
Charlemagne's empire
at his death in 814.
Although illiterate
himself, Charlemagne
was responsible for
great advances in
the promotion of
learning and culture
within his realm.*

CHARLEMAGNE'S EMPIRE IN 814

Frankish
kingdom 768

conquests of
Charlemagne
768–814

dependent
territories 814

unaligned
territories

king married the sons of the Frankish king, but later when the Lombards tried to settle the power struggles between two Frankish leaders, war broke out between the Lombards and the Franks.

The Frankish leader, Charlemagne, conquered Lombard areas in Italy. In Rome, on Christmas Day in AD 800, the pope crowned Charlemagne Holy Roman emperor. His name means Charles the Great. Italy was divided into three parts: Lombardy, the **Papal States** and the south, which was still under Byzantine control. The Lombards and the Franks encouraged loyalty from their followers by using the feudal system. Land was given to noblemen by the king. In return, he expected the noblemen to take an oath to be loyal to him and to pay him money or goods every year. The noblemen had to bring soldiers to fight for the king in times of war. In turn, the nobleman gave parts of his land to others, who promised to be loyal to him.

This illustration from a medieval manuscript – now in the National Library in Turin – depicts Charlemagne's troops laying siege to the city of Rome.

Noblemen had the power of life or death over the people who lived in the areas they controlled. The serfs who worked the land had to do work for their lord. They had no protection or rights if the lord was unjust in the way he treated them and they were not permitted to read or write or make money. Because they were 'tied' to a lord, they were not allowed to move away to try to make a living somewhere else.

THE MARITIME REPUBLICS

Some coastal cities had protected themselves against the invasions after the fall of the Roman empire. They constructed defensive walls, forts and good harbours and built up powerful fleets. By trading goods around the Mediterranean, they brought wealth to Italy.

Beginning in the 9th century, these coastal cities became the maritime republics. The most important were Venice, Pisa, Genoa and, further south, Amalfi. They fought off and defeated pirates from the north African coast, and often set up trading bases a long way from their home cities.

Trade brought not only wealth but also knowledge. Many technical and commercial developments came from the Muslim world, including the use of modern numbers. We incorrectly call them 'Arabic' but they were in fact derived from an Indian script.

For the maritime republics, it was not the conquest of large areas of territory that was important but the control of trading routes and strategic ports throughout the Mediterranean area.

THE MARITIME REPUBLICS

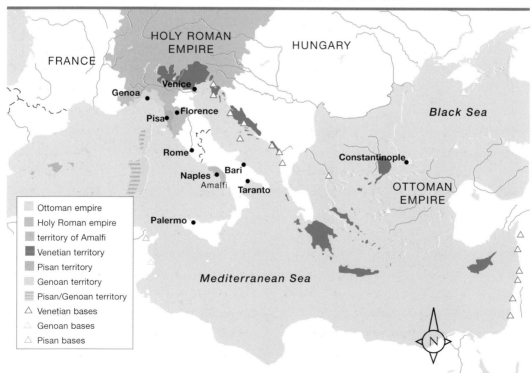

FRANCE

HOLY ROMAN EMPIRE

HUNGARY

Genoa

Venice

Florence

Pisa

Black Sea

Rome

Constantinople

Naples • Bari
Amalfi
Taranto

OTTOMAN EMPIRE

Palermo

Mediterranean Sea

Ottoman empire
Holy Roman empire
territory of Amalfi
Venetian territory
Pisan territory
Genoan territory
Pisan/Genoan territory
△ Venetian bases
△ Genoan bases
△ Pisan bases

N

The Venetian empire

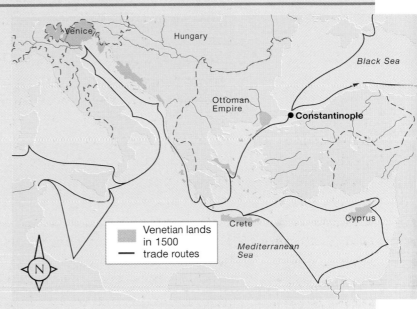

The Most Serene Republic of Venice, or 'La Serenissima', was run by a leader called the **doge** with the help of two advisory councils. People who were thought to be enemies of the republic were put in prison.

Initially, the city owed its allegiance to the Byzantine empire based at Constantinople, and Byzantium granted the city extensive trading rights in the eastern Mediterranean. It was with the trade generated by the Crusades, however, that the city truly came into its own. With the sack of Constantinople in 1204 came effective control of the eastern Mediterranean, further secured by the defeat of its main rival, Genoa, in the War of Chioggia (1379–80).

Venetians were clever business people who were happy to trade with all nations, whatever their religion or politics. At the height of the republic's success, Venetian territories included parts of northern Italy, the Adriatic coast around Venice and, further east, parts of mainland Greece and many of the Aegean islands near Greece, including Crete and Cyprus. The Venetians became famous as plunderers and their art and architecture showed a strong influence from the Middle East.

A Venetian trader, Marco Polo, went as far as China to find out about trade goods such as silk and spices. He was given a position at the Chinese emperor's court and later brought back tales of China in addition to trade goods.

Venetian commerce declined when Europeans landed in the Americas in the late 15th century. The rise of the Ottoman empire led to the loss of territories in the Mediterranean. After 1600, trade began to be centred on Europe's Atlantic ports, not on the Mediterranean. In 1797, Napoleon finally brought the Venetian empire to an end. In 1815, the city passed to the Austrian Hapsburg empire until unification with the rest of Italy.

THE POPE AND THE EMPEROR

From the 10th century on, Rome was the centre of the Christian world. The pope organized the Catholic Church from his territories in central Italy. The pope had crowned the first Holy Roman emperor – a Germanic emperor ruling much of what is now central mainland Europe. However, there were constant struggles between the Church and the Holy Roman emperor. They became rivals as the Church extended its lands and its influence in European politics. The struggles between the empire and the papacy continued for centuries.

During the 11th century, the people living in cities in the north and centre of Italy wanted to live freely. They declared themselves free from the rule of the Holy Roman emperor and the pope, deciding to elect their own judges, make their own laws, have their own currency and create alliances and make war without having to consult any other cities.

Once they had established these rights, the people of a *comune* (city-state) were ready to fight to defend

> Muslim pirates invaded Italy from Africa and Spain and in 846 looted Rome, forcing the pope, Leo IV, to build a defensive wall around the Vatican, which can still be seen today. Muslims settled in Sicily where they remained for 200 years.

The Visconti of Milan

The Visconti family rose to prominence in the 11th century, transforming their family title of 'viscount' into their surname. Pope Urban IV appointed Ottone Visconti archbishop of Milan in 1262, and the head of the Visconti family then acquired the titles of 'vicar' and *signore* (lord) of Milan. During the 13th and 14th centuries, the family made marriage alliances with French and German princes. In the 1350s, the influence of the Visconti stretched as far as the cities of Genoa and Bologna. During this period, the family was also involved in wars with the popes and with the city-state of Florence. By the beginning of the 15th century, the Visconti ruled most of northern Italy with the exception of Venice and Florence – Pisa, Siena, Bologna and Perugia all lay under Visconti control. This was also a period of great artistic patronage: the poet Petrarch was a member of the Visconti court. In 1447, the Venetian army marched on Milan and Filippo Maria Visconti appealed to his son-in-law, the mercenary Francesco Sforza, for help. The city was defended, and on Filippo Maria's death, the Visconti state passed to Sforza.

them. Sometimes there were difficulties when the citizens of the *comune* could not agree among themselves and split into groups, or when nearby towns supported different sides. Two of the best-known political parties were the Guelfs (supporters of the pope) and the Ghibellines (supporters of the emperor). Fighting between the city-states allowed tyrannical rulers to take power. A powerful family could rule a city-state for years. The Visconti family ruled Milan (see opposite), the Della Scala in Verona, the Gonzagas in Mantua and the Medici in Florence.

Some cities paid mercenaries to protect them from the bandits who also roamed the land. These groups of paid soldiers were led by a *condottiere*, who negotiated the contract for protection.

In the south of Italy, the situation was different. Sicily had been invaded and settled by Muslims in the 9th and 10th centuries. The Normans had pushed the Saracens out in the 11th and 12th centuries and established the Kingdom of the Two Sicilies. Cities such as Naples and other territories in southern Italy were added by conquest. Emperor Frederick II inherited Sicily in 1198 and wanted to control all of Italy.

When he died, the pope gave his kingdom to the brother of the king of France. In 1282, a revolt broke out and a 30-year war – the War of the Sicilian Vespers – started. The Sicilians turned to the Spanish for help. The Spanish beat the French and took over Sicily.

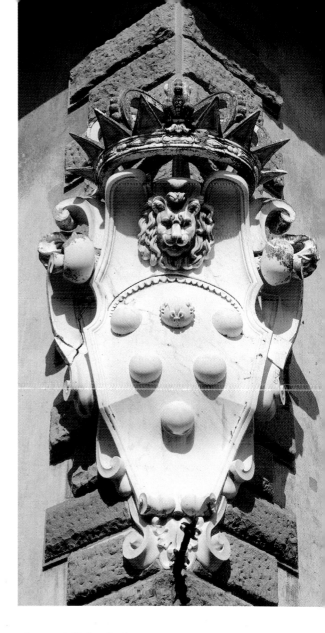

The crest of the six Medici balls can be found on many buildings in Pisa and Siena, wealthy cities that became vassals of the Florentine family firm.

THE RENAISSANCE

By the end of the 14th century, many city-states – including Milan, Bologna, Florence, Mantua and Verona – had established their independence. Like the maritime republics, the city-states became important trade centres.

With money from trade, wealthy families were able to build fine houses and public buildings. The **Gothic**-style **cathedral** in Milan was started in 1396. In Florence, sculptors and artists worked on decorating the **Palazzo** Vecchio for the ruling Medici family (see below).

Inspired by the art and philosophy of the Romans and the Greeks, many artists explored new ideas. Beginning in Italy and then spreading to other countries, this revival in learning was called the *Rinascimento*, meaning 'rebirth'. We use the French word 'Renaissance' for it. It lasted throughout the 15th and 16th centuries.

There were also many discoveries in science and advances in technology. The dukes of Florence, for example, set up a society of astronomers and other scientists.

The lavish decoration of the Sala dei Gigli in the Palazzo Vecchio in Florence shows the extent of patronage (support of artists) by Italy's ruling families. The fresco here is by Domenico Ghirlandaio and was painted in about 1482.

In the bank

As Italian city-states developed their trade, they organized systems for making payments in different countries and continents. This meant that merchants did not have to travel around with large, heavy bags of gold or silver coins and risk being robbed on their journey. Traders used a system of bills of exchange, which could be changed for a certain amount of money like traveller's cheques (see right).

Many terms in modern banking have an Italian origin, even the word 'bank'. It comes from *banca*, the table or bench that was used as a counter in a trading office. Italian traders from Genoa, Florence, Venice and Siena also developed a sophisticated bookkeeping system for their accounts.

ITALIAN EXPLORERS

Explorers from Italian cities went to many corners of the world. Christopher Columbus, a navigator from Genoa, was sure that by crossing the Atlantic and continuing west he could reach India. Venetian traders had travelled overland to India to bring back spices, perfumes, scented wood and precious stones. In the 15th century, war between the Turks and the Venetians made this journey impossible.

Columbus explained his idea to people in Genoa and Naples, even to the pope, but they were not interested. Finally, King Ferdinand and Queen Isabella of Spain sponsored him. With three small ships, the *Niña*, the *Pinta* and the *Santa María*, he set off from southern Spain on 3 August 1492.

After a long and exhausting voyage, the ships reached the shores of a new land on 12 October. Columbus called the people he found there 'Indians' because he thought he was in India. Only after more voyages did Columbus realize that he had reached a 'new world'. Later, another Italian, Amerigo Vespucci (1454–1512), explored the coast of South America. The name for the Americas comes from a Latin version of his first name, Americus. Further north, the Venetian Giovanni Caboto (1450–99), known as John Cabot, explored the coast of present-day Canada for the king of England, Henry VII.

Columbus' voyage to America was a product of the advances in seamanship made by the trading city-states of Genoa, Pisa and Venice during the 14th and 15th centuries.

A BATTLEGROUND

In the 16th century, Italy was a collection of city-states and kingdoms that were often controlled by foreign powers. In 1530, the Spanish king, who was also the Holy Roman emperor, controlled many areas of Italy. Milan and parts of Tuscany, in addition to Naples, Sicily and Sardinia, were under his control. Venice, Genoa, Mantua, Savoy and the Papal States were still independent. The time would come, however, when Italy's rich trading routes would become irresistible to the central European powers and previously independent areas would be merged together.

THE ITALIAN STATES IN 1454

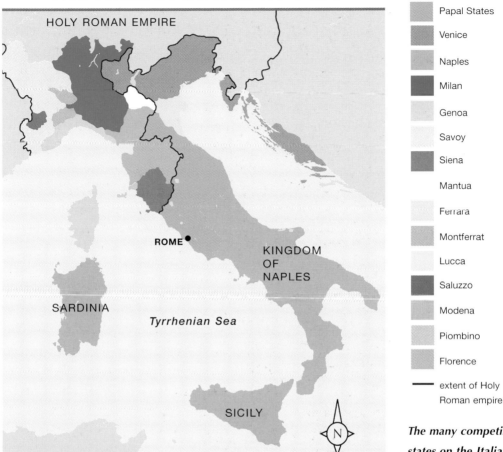

	Papal States
	Venice
	Naples
	Milan
	Genoa
	Savoy
	Siena
	Mantua
	Ferrara
	Montferrat
	Lucca
	Saluzzo
	Modena
	Piombino
	Florence
▬	extent of Holy Roman empire

The many competing states on the Italian peninsula in the 15th century made the region vulnerable to attack from foreign powers.

During the 17th century, the peninsula of Italy became a battleground for different European powers who wanted to conquer the country. Economic power passed away from the Italian city-states to the European powers establishing overseas colonies. In the Thirty Years' War (1618–48) and the War of the Spanish Succession (1701–14), areas of Italy passed from one power to another. The Austrians, French and Spanish sent their armies to fight each other. Lombardy, Mantua, Naples and Sardinia fell under Austrian control, while Piedmont passed to the Duke of Savoy. In the mid-1730s, the last of the Medici died and Tuscany

The grand tour

A taste for all things classical had been gathering steam in Europe throughout the early 18th century. However, it was the discovery of the buried town of Pompeii outside Naples in 1748 that really fired the enthusiasm of educated Europeans for relics of the Roman empire. During the mid-18th century, Italy began to be popular as a destination for the younger members of the European aristocracy. Young people's education was felt to be incomplete until they had savoured the classical delights of Greece and Rome, and the elegant ruins inspired the Romantic imagination. Wealthier visitors were able to buy up large amounts of statuary, frescoes and even entire buildings. Rome became the main destination for a tour of the classical sites – the grand tour.

Napoleon's coronation as king of Italy turned into a stand-off with Pope Pius VII. Insulted at being summoned to Paris, the pope arrived days late. So annoyed was Napoleon that, when it came to the coronation, he snatched the crown from Pius and crowned himself.

passed to the French house of Lorraine. In the latter half of the 18th century, much of northern Italy was controlled by Austria, while the south lay largely under Bourbon control.

It was only with the rise of the French leader Napoleon Bonaparte towards the end of the 18th century that **nationalism** began in earnest. French armies invaded northern Italy in 1796 and set up a series of republics. The Cisalpine republic had its capital at Milan and the Ligurian republic at Genoa. There was also a Roman republic in Rome and a Parthenopean republic, centred on Naples. Later, Napoleon made these areas into an Italian kingdom and made himself king in 1806. This state of affairs lasted until 1815, when Bonaparte was defeated at the Battle of Waterloo and his empire was dismantled.

Italy was divided up again. The Austrians took Lombardy and Venice. Piedmont-Sardinia in the northwest became an independent kingdom. The Spanish controlled the Kingdom of the Two Sicilies (Sicily and the area of the Italian peninsula south of the Papal States) and the pope ruled in the Papal States.

UNITED ITALY

Although Italy had not been united since the time of the Romans, Italians were influenced by the ideas of liberty from the French Revolution and wanted to unite their country. Three men were central in the struggle to free Italy and make it a nation.

Giuseppe Mazzini (1805–72) wrote articles about political freedom and joined one of the secret societies that promoted a united Italy. He was put in prison, but on his release was even more determined to help his country. In 1831, he set up the Young Italy movement. After a failed revolt, Mazzini was sent into exile in London.

While Mazzini was trying to inspire people to fight for a united Italy, Count Camillo Cavour (1810–61) founded a newspaper called *Il Risorgimento* (the Resurrection) in Piedmont. The name of his newspaper was later taken for the movement to unify Italy. There were many revolutions across Europe in 1848, and Cavour joined people from Lombardy and Venice who were fighting the Austrian empire. They failed, but Vittorio Emanuele II, who was king of Piedmont-Sardinia, made Cavour chief minister. With the help of the French, in 1859 the Piedmontese army defeated the Austrians at the battles of Magenta and Solferino.

The third principal figure in the *Risorgimento* was Giuseppe Garibaldi (1807–82). Because of his association with Mazzini, he had to leave Italy and spent many years in the USA and in South America. In 1854, he came back and fought with the king of Piedmont-Sardinia's army against the Austrians.

As Vittorio Emmanuele's army moved towards the south, Garibaldi went to Sicily in 1860. He landed with 1000 volunteers, who took the island. The army then

Garibaldi, the leader of the Italian nationalist movement, was actually born in Nice, now in France, and spent twelve years in Uruguay before returning to Italy to fight in the republican army.

While Garibaldi travelled to Sicily to launch an attack from the south, Cavour and Vittorio Emmanuele marched Piedmontese troops down the peninsula. Only after France had been defeated by the Prussians, and the French had been ousted from Rome, did the city become the Italian capital in 1871.

territory ceded to other states

Italy 1861

battles

route of Garibaldi's Thousand, 1860

route of Vittorio Emmanuele II, 1860

THE FIGHT FOR INDEPENDENCE

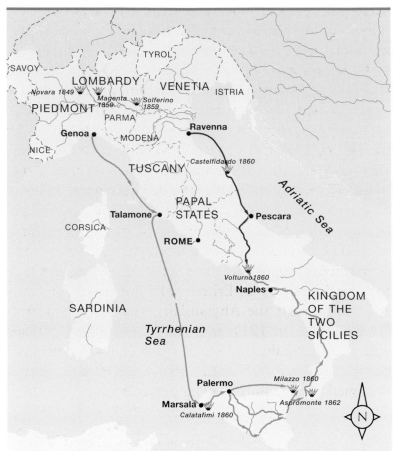

marched north and captured Naples. The two armies met at Teano on 26 October. Vittorio Emmanuele was proclaimed king of Italy, and Turin became the capital. By 1861, almost all of Italy was united. Five years later, the Austrians gave up Venice, and finally in 1870 the pope allowed the Papal States to become part of Italy. Italy was a country again, with its capital in Rome.

MAKING A NATION

Italy was united, but people had very different ideas about what kind of country they wanted. At first, many politicians concentrated more on the problems of making Italy a nation. Among others things, they had to organize the administrative and legal system, the postal service and state schools. The national road and railway networks were expanded. To finance all of this, high taxes had to be imposed on the people.

Garibaldi was keen to see a lot of social reforms. In 1876, a more **left-wing** government introduced five years of free, compulsory primary-school education. The voting system was reformed, so that anyone who had studied at primary school could vote. At the same time, industry was developing in Italy. Workers organized themselves into groups to demand better rights.

Abroad, Italy began to expand its trade with Africa. It became more ambitious and tried to take over territory in Abyssinia (now known as Ethiopia). The Abyssinians fought back, and the Italians were left with the small territory of Eritrea. The Somalis asked Italy for help against the Abyssinians, and Italy took over Somalia, too. In 1911 and 1912, the Italians invaded and occupied Libya. None of these conquests brought the wealth the Italians had hoped for, as the areas they occupied were mainly poor or desert lands.

The international situation

The isolation of the new Italian state during the 1870s was made more severe by the French occupation of Tunisia in 1881. Dissatisfaction with France led the Italians to form an alliance with Germany and the Austro-Hungarian empire in 1882. The alliance secured Italian interests in the Mediterranean against French expansion, but Italian imperialist ambitions now turned to north Africa. These can be seen as part of the European powers' 'Scramble for Africa' – the eagerness of the industrialized powers to establish colonies providing raw materials to feed the factories that supported their economies. Despite Italian raids into east Africa in 1889, a full-scale Italo-French conflict was averted by an agreement in 1902 that effectively gave each country a separate sphere of influence. This resulted in the Italian invasion of Libya in 1911 and the Italo-Turkish War of 1911–12. Eventually, however, the earlier alliance with Germany and Austria was to bring about a far greater penalty for the Italian nation.

A WORLD WAR

Pope Pius IX initially refused to recognize the Kingdom of Italy and was stripped of his governmental powers and of the Quirinale Palace. It was only with the accession to power of the Fascist Party that the papacy regained its self-government.

Italian troops of the 35th infantry division marching in 1916.

In 1882, Italy had become part of the Triple Alliance with two important powers of central and northern Europe: Germany and Austria. The other major European powers – Russia, France and Britain – formed another alliance.

Within the German and Austrian empires, there were people of other ethnic origins who wanted to be independent. On 28 June 1914, a Serb nationalist named Gavrilo Princip assassinated Archduke Franz Ferdinand, who was the heir to the Austrian empire. Austria held the Serbian government responsible and declared war.

The war might not have lasted long if the Russians had not become involved. Austria's ally, Germany, also declared war on Serbia, Russia and its ally, France. Britain came to support France. World War One had begun.

Italy stayed neutral until 1915, when it declared war on Austria and Germany. The Italians hoped to win back territories in Austria that had large Italian populations, which they thought should join Italy.

The Italians fought along the Alps, sheltering from the intense cold in trenches. The hardest fighting took place in June 1918, but in October the Italian soldiers beat the Germans at the battle of Vittorio Veneto.

MUSSOLINI

After World War One, Europe went through difficult times. In Russia, there was a revolution and a **communist** government took over. Italy had to face serious financial problems and jobs became hard to find. Many ordinary people thought life would be better if they had a **socialist** or communist system. The Popular Party and the socialists were the two main parties in the 1919 elections, but neither had a majority in parliament.

Another political movement developed: fascism. The leader was Benito Mussolini (1883–1945), who was an ex-socialist. Many of the fascists were ex-soldiers who could not get used to peace again and opposed the socialists. In 1922, the fascists marched on Rome, and King Vittorio Emmanuele III asked Mussolini to head the government.

Mussolini quickly became a dictator and banned legal opposition in parliament. Special squads threatened people who opposed Mussolini. The Italian parliament had almost no power. In 1936, Mussolini invaded Ethiopia once again to find a source of the raw materials that Italy lacked and to find markets for its goods.

At the same time, other dictators were taking control in Germany and in Spain. In 1938, Germany occupied its neighbour Austria and parts of Czechoslovakia. In 1939, Germany attacked Poland. France and Britain

Benito Mussolini was born at Predappio near Rimini and worked as a journalist, founding his own newspaper, Il Popolo d'Italia (The Italian People), before forming the Italian Fascist Party in 1921.

declared war on Germany. Italy was Germany's ally and declared war on Greece. World War Two had started.

After the Japanese bombed the US naval base at Pearl Harbor, the USA entered the war on the side of the Allies. Italian and German armies in Africa were defeated by British and American soldiers, who moved on to Sicily. In Italy, power was given back to the king and Mussolini was arrested. The Italians joined the side of the Allies. By the end of 1943, the south of Italy was under the control of British and American soldiers, while the north was occupied by the Germans. Some Italians became partisans, part of a secret army that hid in woods and mountains and fought against the Germans. Mussolini tried to escape to Switzerland but he was caught and shot. The war in Europe ended in May 1945.

Italian partisans in northern Italy bearing the Italian flag in February 1945.

A NEW REPUBLIC

After the war, Italy had to give up its African colonies. Part of Piedmont was given to France, and Istria to the east became part of Yugoslavia. In 1946, the Italians voted in a referendum to become a republic.

The first government after the war was dominated by the Christian Democrat Party led by Alcide De Gasperi (1881–1954), who won more than half the vote, but it also included members of the Socialist and Communist parties in a coalition. In 1947, De Gasperi formed a government that excluded socialists and communists.

During World War Two, bombing and fighting had destroyed towns, railways, bridges, factories and ports. Aid from the USA helped with machinery and raw materials for rebuilding the country.

Italian people worked hard to put the postwar years behind them and the standard of living improved. The Italian government set up a special fund – the *Cassa del Mezzogiorno* (State Fund for the South) – to help develop the south of Italy. In 1957, Italy joined the European Economic Community with West Germany, France, Belgium, Luxembourg and the Netherlands. By the 1960s, industry in the north of the country began to boom, particularly the car industry, and many people migrated from the poorer agricultural regions of the south to the booming cities of the north, such as Milan and Turin.

Former prime minister Aldo Moro is held hostage in 1976 by the Red Brigades. His body was later found in a car in the centre of Rome equidistant from the headquarters of the two main political parties.

The Christian Democrat Party held power for nearly 50 years after World War Two. However, the Communist Party formed an important opposition, with millions of members. During the late 1960s, there were many student protests in Italy and in 1969 came the *Autumno Caldo* (Hot Autumn), a period of strikes and unrest that continued into 1971.

The 1970s and the 1980s were marked by the rise of terrorism in Italy. **Right-wing** and left-wing groups were active. Neofascist groups planted bombs. In 1980, 84 people were killed in an explo-

sion at the Bologna railway station. Some extreme left-wing activists formed the Red Brigades (*Brigate Rosse*) and other groups. They wanted to break up the right-wing Christian Democrats' monopoly of political power in Italy and improve social conditions. Business people, judges, university professors, a NATO general and even an ex-prime minister, Aldo Moro (see above), were kidnapped or assassinated by the Red Brigades as a means of protesting against political inaction.

The years between 1973 and 1980 in Italy, the years of terrorism, were known as the *Anni di Piombo* (Years of Lead).

The *Partito Demo-cratico della Sinistra* (PDS) took on many of the symbols of the old Italian Communist Party, including that of the oak tree.

In 1983, declining support for the Christian Democrats led them to enter into a coalition with the socialists, and the country had its first socialist prime minister, Bettino Craxi (1934–99). In the early 1990s, after the fall of communism in the former Soviet Union and eastern Europe, the Italian Communist Party split into two parts, the larger part (later the **PDS**, see left) abandoning many of the central policies of communism, with the smaller faction (*Rifondazione Communista*, Refounded Communists) sticking to its earlier principles.

The mafia

The **mafia** has a long history in Italy. First emerging in Sicily in medieval times, it began as a secret society attempting to throw off the yoke of the island's foreign rulers. The mafia took its name from the small private armies, or *mafie,* used by absentee landlords to protect their possessions. So harsh were the landowners that the mafia gained substantial support from the local people. The mafia's code of behaviour was based on *omertà,* the principle of never helping the authorities in the detection of crimes, nor giving evidence against others. Revenge could be taken only by the victim of the crime.

By the early 20th century, 'families' or groups of **mafiosi** controlled much of the economy of southern Italy. Mussolini's fascists nearly crushed the mafia by imprisoning many of its leaders. At the end of World War Two, however, US occupation authorities released many of the *mafiosi* and the mafia began to take hold of emerging Italian industry in the south. During the later 20th century, huge sums from public works were siphoned off into mafia accounts, and cities such as Naples and Palermo were effectively controlled by *mafiosi*. It had long been accepted that the influence of the mafia spread to the highest level of Italian politics. In the early 1990s, corruption scandals and confessions from captured mafia bosses linked the mafia with the former prime minister Giulio Andreotti, who had been virtually a permanent fixture in Italian politics since the war. In 1992, within two months, two judges, Giovanni Falcone and Paolo Borsellino, were murdered. Giovanni Falcone's car was blown up on a motorway, killing the judge, his wife, the driver and three police officers.

Since the 1980s, the mafia has monopolized the drug trade in Italy. It still controls large areas of the south and has recently moved into the former communist economies of eastern Europe.

The *Lega Nord*

The *Lega Nord* (Northern League) first achieved electoral success in 1992, gaining 7% of the vote with their anti-corruption platform. The party was formed to oppose what it saw as the subsidizing of the poor south by the richer north. The league's leader, Umberto Bossi, has called for the establishment of a separate state called Padania in northern Italy, consisting of Veneto, Liguria Piedmont, Lombardy, Emilia-Romagna and the small **Alpine** regions. He has advised northern Italians to withhold taxes from what he sees as the corrupt bureaucracy of Rome and the league has minted its own coin. Despite support for the league – in 1996 it gained 9% of the vote – most Italians strongly oppose division of their country. Bossi's portrayal of the south as corrupt was undermined by the *Tangentopoli* scandals unearthed in Milan, the league's home town (see below).

TANGENTOPOLI AND ITS AFTERMATH

The major event of the last decade has been the unfolding of the *Tangentopoli* scandals. The Italian word for a bribe is a '*tangente*', and Italians called Milan, the centre of the initial scandal, *Tangentopoli*. In 1992, a judge from Milan, Antonio di Pietro, started an investigation into corruption among politicians and business people who had accepted bribes in exchange for public works' contracts worth millions of pounds. This investigation was called Operation *Mani Pulite* (Clean Hands).

The corruption reached to the heart of the Italian political establishment and members of almost all parties connected with government were implicated. In the national elections of 1994, support for the main political parties, particularly the Christian Democrats and the socialists, collapsed. As a result, the right-wing alliance known as the *Polo della Libertà* (Freedom Alliance) came to power. It was composed of the neo-fascist *Alleanza Nazionale* (National Alliance), the *Lega Nord* (Northern League, see box) and *Forza Italia* (Go Italy). The latter was led by the media tycoon Silvio Berlusconi (born 1936). The coalition collapsed after a matter of months. In the 1996 election, a centre-left

Two years after becoming prime minister in 1994, Silvio Berlusconi himself came under investigation for corruption. A large number of charges were dismissed because of the lengthy process they took to pass through Italy's courts.

Italy's prime ministers since World War Two:
- A. De Gasperi (1946–53)
- G. Pella (1953–54)
- A. Fanfani (1954)
- M. Scelba (1954–55)
- A. Segni (1955–57)
- A. Zoli (1957–58)
- A. Fanfani (1958–59)
- A. Segni (1959–60)
- F. Tambroni (1960)
- A. Fanfani (1960–63)
- G. Leone (1963)
- A. Moro (1963–68)

coalition known as the Olive Tree Alliance won a majority led by the former professor Romano Prodi (born 1940). In the 2001 elections, Silvio Berlusconi was again elected to power as prime minister, even though he had been investigated for corruption in 1996.

POLITICAL ORGANIZATION

Italy is a **democratic** republic. The head of government is the prime minister, who is referred to in Italy as the President of the Council of Ministers. The prime minister chooses the government ministers and directs government policy. The head of state is the president, whose role is largely ceremonial, although the position can involve important constitutional duties. This was particularly evident in the aftermath of the *Mani Pulite* investigation in 1994, when most of the Italian political establishment had been discredited and again after the fall of Berlusconi's government in the following year. After the fall of Berlusconi's government, Oscar Scalfaro appointed a caretaker team of adminstrators to run the country. It was clearly important that the president should be seen to be above party political bias in such a situation.

Italy's parliament is split into two chambers. Of the 315 seats in the upper house, the Senate, 232 are directly elected and 83 are elected by regional proportional representation. There are also a number of senators for

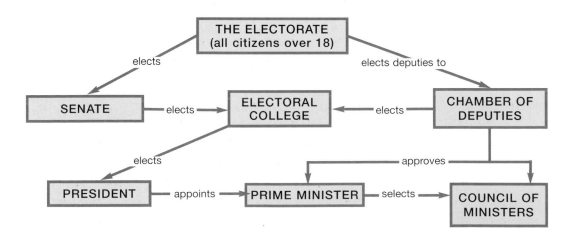

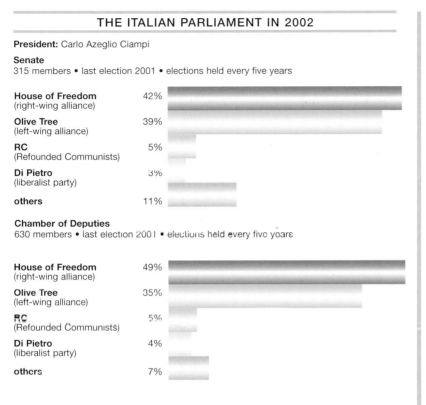

THE ITALIAN PARLIAMENT IN 2002

President: Carlo Azeglio Ciampi

Senate
315 members • last election 2001 • elections held every five years

House of Freedom (right-wing alliance)	42%	
Olive Tree (left-wing alliance)	39%	
RC (Refounded Communists)	5%	
Di Pietro (liberalist party)	3%	
others	11%	

Chamber of Deputies
630 members • last election 2001 • elections held every five years

House of Freedom (right-wing alliance)	49%	
Olive Tree (left-wing alliance)	35%	
RC (Refounded Communists)	5%	
Di Pietro (liberalist party)	4%	
others	7%	

life, who include former presidents and leading figures from the establishment – these currently include the heads of the Fiat and Benetton companies. Senators are elected for five-year terms. Of the 630 seats in the **Chamber of Deputies**, 475 are directly elected and 155 are elected by proportional representation. Again, members serve five-year terms. The difference between the system of direct election and proportional representation is that, with the former, the candidate with the largest proportion of the vote in a constituency wins the seat and other candidates do not win anything; in the latter, seats are allotted according to a party's proportion of the vote in the whole country, so even if a party comes second in a number of constituencies, it will still win some seats. The former system aims to give a solid majority to one party while the latter aims to give a fair distribution of seats to the parties. The Italian system is an attempt to obtain the best of both systems.

- G. Leone (1968)
- M. Rumor (1968–70)
- E. Colombo (1970–72)
- G. Andreotti (1972–74)
- A. Moro (1974–76)
- G. Andreotti (1976–78)
- F. Cossiga (1979–80)
- A. Forlani (1980–81)
- G. Spadolini (1981–82)
- A. Fanfani (1982–83)
- B. Craxi (1983–87)
- A. Fanfani (1987)
- G. Goria (1987–88)
- C. De Mita (1988–89)
- G. Andreotti (1989–92)
- G. Amato (1992–94)
- S. Berlusconi (1994)
- L. Dini (1994–96)
- R. Prodi (1996–98)
- M. D'Alema (1998–2000)
- G. Amato (2000–01)
- S. Berlusconi (2001–)

The economy

'An untouchable and sacred state institution, on a par with royalty, the church, a regime.'

Italian dictator Benito Mussolini on the Fiat car company

During the second half of the 20th century, Italy moved from being a largely agricultural country to being one of the world's major economic powers. This was achieved through its inventive business people, designers and engineers, who have adapted quickly to changes in world markets. Italy is famous for many different products, ranging from clothing and leather goods to agricultural products, although its main exports are now industrial machinery and textiles. The country is unusual among major industrial nations in that much of its industry is based on smaller family firms that export quality products with a specific market. In recent years, the country has made huge strides to overcome its public debt and problems with inflation in order to meet the criteria needed for entry into the common European currency, the euro, which replaced the Italian lira in 2002.

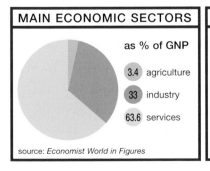

MAIN ECONOMIC SECTORS

as % of GNP

- 3.4 agriculture
- 33 industry
- 63.6 services

source: *Economist World in Figures*

THE WORKFORCE

as % of workforce

- 7 agriculture
- 41 industry
- 52 services

source: *Economist World in Figures*

Italy produces more wine than any other country. Even steep terrain is used, split into terraces, like these hills on the Amalfi coast south of Naples.

MAIN TRADING PARTNERS

EXPORTS		IMPORTS	
%		%	
16.4	Germany	18	Germany
12.2	France	13.2	France
7.9	USA	6.7	United Kingdom
7.1	United Kingdom	6.2	Netherlands
5.2	Spain	5	USA
51.2	others	50.9	others

source: *Economist World in Figures*

Large and small business

Italy is unusual for a modern industrial country because it has many small and medium-sized companies and relatively few large ones. About 90 per cent of Italian companies employ between 11 and 500 people, often with fewer rather than more workers.

Smaller businesses are often more flexible than some larger companies. When times are hard, they can scale down their activities, and when things get better, they can sometimes respond more quickly to changes in the economy.

Families are important in business. Many of the smaller companies are run by families. Some large industrial groups are strongly identified with the families that founded them, such as the Agnellis who set up the car giant Fiat in Turin. Some of the smaller companies work directly for the large ones. For example, they may specialize in one product or part of a production process needed by the vehicle industry.

Other small businesses are more independent and successfully export their own products to other countries. About 40 per cent of companies with fewer than 50 employees depend on exports for the majority of their earnings.

The big companies are mainly concentrated in northern Italy, especially in the area between Milan, Turin and Genoa. Milan is Italy's financial and industrial centre. It is also home to Italy's fashion industry.

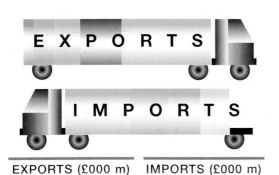

EXPORTS (£000 m)		IMPORTS (£000 m)	
engineering products	53.1	engineering products	30.6
textiles and clothing	24.5	chemicals	18.2
transport equipment	14.6	transport equipment and parts	15.8
chemicals	12.8	energy products	13.7
food and drink	6.1		
total (including others)	148.9	total (including others)	130.2

source: *Economist World in Figures*

Textiles and clothing form Italy's second-largest export in terms of revenue. When the European Economic Community (EEC), the first economic association of European countries, was set up in 1957, Italy was one of the original members. In 1993, Italy was one of the fifteen countries that formed the **European Union** (EU), which allowed political cooperation and free trade between its members.

EUROPEAN UNION

European Union member countries

non-member countries

Being a member of the EU is very important for Italy. The EU is Italy's largest trading partner. The country sends 55 per cent of its exports there, and takes 60 per cent of its imports from the EU. The USA is the next largest export market, making up approximately 8 per cent of the total.

There are plans to expand the current EU of fifteen countries to include several eastern European countries, such as Poland and the Czech Republic, in 2004.

North and south

The richest regions of Italy are all in northern and central Italy. Southern Italy generates only about one-fifth of tax revenues, although 35 per cent of public spending goes to the south. (Government spending is calculated according to the size of the population.) Twenty-six per cent of people in the south are considered poor – those with an income less than half the average income per person – against 9 per cent in northern and central Italy.

In 1950, a special fund called the *Cassa del Mezzogiorno* (State Fund for the South) was set up to help develop the south. Money from the fund was used to modernize agriculture, create industrial zones and improve infrastructure by building 2000 kilometres (1240 miles) of motorways and by modernizing ports. Agricultural output doubled within twenty years. Some large corporations, including steel and car manufacturers, set up plants in cities such as Taranto, Naples and Bari.

Despite this large investment, the south still has a much higher level of unemployment than the north. The average for the whole country is about 11 per cent, but in the south it is 21.7 per cent.

Finding a job is especially difficult in the south where 33.8 per cent of 15 to 24-year-olds are without work. Since many young people go to university first, then look for their first job, there are high levels of unemployed graduates. In some areas, up to 80 per cent of people looking for work are graduates.

In northern and central Italy, young people take temporary jobs as a stepping stone to permanent employment. In the south, young job seekers often reject temporary low-status jobs, which are poorly paid, as they worry about not being able to move on to a better job. They look for government jobs, which are permanent, steady and better paid. For example, up to 20 per cent of Sicily's workforce work for the government in universities, government offices, museums or historic sites.

On the move

One of the ways in which people escaped from lack of opportunity, especially in the south, was to move away. Between 1861 and 1973, 26 million Italians left Italy. It was only in 1973, for the first time in Italy's recent history, that more Italians returned than left the country.

The first large groups of emigrants left northern Italy in the 1860s, followed later by millions of southerners. Emigrants went to South America, settling in countries such as Argentina, Brazil and Uruguay, but the majority went to live in the USA. After World War Two, Italians looked for work in European countries, such as Switzerland, France and Germany.

In the 1950s and 1960s, there was a great wave of migration within Italy. Many people moved from the south to work in the new factories around Milan, Turin, Genoa and Bologna. There were no language problems and it was easier to take the family along. Even today, young people still move from the poorer regions of the south in search of work.

Farming and fishing

About 7 per cent of Italians work in agriculture. They cultivate the 40 per cent of Italy's land area devoted to farming. Many farms are small: about 75 per cent cover 5 hectares (12 acres) or less. The larger, more modern farms are mainly in northern and central Italy, especially in the Po Valley. Despite the efforts of the Italian government to improve farming, mountain areas and parts of the south are still fairly unproductive.

One of the most valuable crops is grapes. Most of them are used for making wine. Better wines have the words *Denominazione di Origine Controllata*, or DOC, on the labels. This indicates a good-quality wine that comes from one wine-making area. Olives are grown mainly in the centre and the south. They are also processed to make olive oil. Some of the top-quality brands are also categorized as DOC oils. Just like wine, the flavour of olive oil varies from one area to another, depending on the soil and climate conditions.

Other major fruit and vegetable produce includes oranges, lemons, peaches, apples and tomatoes. Sicily produces about 60 per cent of all citrus fruits grown in Italy. Sugar beet is also produced on a wide scale.

A crop not immediately associated with Italy is rice. It is grown in large, water-logged fields around

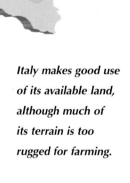

HOW ITALY USES ITS LAND

crop land

forest

pasture

mountains

Italy makes good use of its available land, although much of its terrain is too rugged for farming.

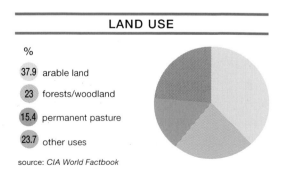

LAND USE

%	
37.9	arable land
23	forests/woodland
15.4	permanent pasture
23.7	other uses

source: *CIA World Factbook*

Men in northern Italy operate an olive press, producing quality olive oil for Italy's export market.

Vercelli and Novara in north-west Italy. This area accounts for about 60 per cent of Italian rice production. Maize and wheat are important grain crops.

There are problems with irrigating food crops. In some areas, especially further south, there is a shortage of water; in others, there are difficulties because of water pollution or because the available water is too salty.

Cattle are raised for meat and milk, especially in the north and the centre. Large numbers of other animals, such as pigs, chickens and sheep, are raised for meat. The country still has to import meat from other countries, however, because Italian people eat more meat than the country's farmers can supply.

Although Italy is surrounded by sea and Italians love to eat fish and seafood, fishing is not a very important economic activity. About half the catch comes from the Adriatic, but fish stocks are low because of the use of drift-nets, which catch undersized or young fish before they can mature and breed. Italian fishing fleets also work further away in the Mediterranean and even the Atlantic. Around Sicily, tuna, anchovies and sardines are caught.

Mineral resources and energy

Italy has very little oil, but what there is lies mostly in the Po Valley, Calabria and Sicily. There are also some natural gas reserves. The country has to import about 75 per cent of its energy requirements, mainly oil and gas from north Africa. The possibility of using nuclear power as a major source of energy supply was abandoned after the Italian people overwhelmingly voted against the idea in a referendum in 1987.

Oil provides about half of the country's energy needs, and about 85 per cent of Italian electricity power stations burn oil. About 17 per cent of electricity is generated in hydroelectric power stations. These are mostly in the Alps in the north, with some stations in the Apennines.

Many raw materials needed for industrial production are also imported. Some minerals are mined, including mercury, pyrites (a source of sulphur), iron ore, potash, zinc, lead and salt. One famous mineral export from Italy is the high-quality white marble from quarries in the Apennines at Carrara in Tuscany. Michelangelo (see page 98) used to come to Carrara to choose blocks for his sculptures, and modern sculptors still visit the quarry today.

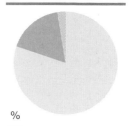

ENERGY SOURCES

%

80.2 fossil fuels (coal, gas, oil)

17.3 hydroelectric power

2.5 other

source: *CIA World Fact Book*

Dependence on imported fossil fuels makes Italy's economy very vulnerable to changes in world oil prices.

Industry

Manufacturing accounts for nearly 20 per cent of Italy's gross national product (GNP). About 40 per cent of Italians work in industry. Machine tools, textile machinery and industrial robots from the mechanical engineering industry are key exports. The textile and leather-working sector is also important, producing clothes and fashion accessories for sale around the world.

United colours

Some Italian companies started small and grew. One of the largest corporations in the textile and clothing sector began as a small company run by the Benetton family. It was based at Ponzano Veneto in the north-eastern province of Treviso. Set up in 1965, it now sells clothes worldwide through a chain of shops. The company began by subcontracting the making of clothes to a number of smaller companies in the local Veneto area, managing the production with sophisticated computerized control of stocks and payment.

Style leaders

Most Italians like to look fashionable, even if they are just going out for a stroll, a coffee with friends or shopping. Some people are so interested in fashion that they wear only designer labels. They are called *firmati* (signed) because they wear clothes with a designer name. The Italian fashion industry, with its twice-yearly shows, is based around the city of Milan. Famous Italian fashion designers include Gucci, Prada, Versace, Armani, Dolce e Gabbana and Valentino.

At home, many Italians like to buy stylish designer furniture or houseware. One company set up by the Alessi family produces a whole range of tableware and kitchenware. Italian design is widely acknowledged as a world leader. This development even extends to the styling of high-performance cars and motorcycles, which are automatically linked with the luxury products of Enzo Ferrari, Ferrucio Lamborghini, Adriano Ducati and Fabio Taglioni.

Food-processing, based on the agricultural crops grown in Italy, is the country's third-largest industrial sector. Other important industries include petroleum products, cars and chemicals. Electrical products include electronic equipment for business and military use. The non-electrical goods sector produces domestic appliances, such as refrigerators, washing machines and dishwashers. The Italian government has a share in many large industrial corporations, including shipyards, steelworks and car factories. It even owns a food-processing company.

The car giant Fiat also produces aircraft engines and telecommunications equipment and has recently developed interests in biological science.

Services

More than 60 per cent of Italians work in service industries, especially in retailing, hotels and restaurants. The government also employs a large number of people – 12 per cent of workers have government jobs. The computer software sector employs 162,000 people.

Tourism generates income for many regions of Italy, and is especially welcome in the poorer areas. As many

MAJOR INDUSTRIES

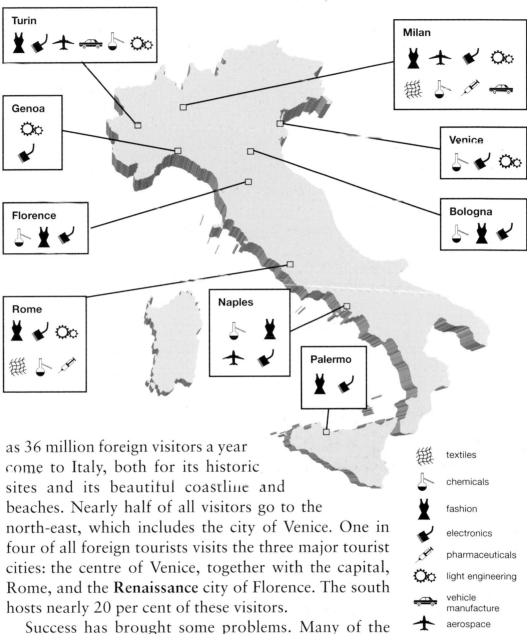

Turin

Milan

Genoa

Venice

Florence

Bologna

Rome

Naples

Palermo

textiles

chemicals

fashion

electronics

pharmaceuticals

light engineering

vehicle manufacture

aerospace

as 36 million foreign visitors a year come to Italy, both for its historic sites and its beautiful coastline and beaches. Nearly half of all visitors go to the north-east, which includes the city of Venice. One in four of all foreign tourists visits the three major tourist cities: the centre of Venice, together with the capital, Rome, and the **Renaissance** city of Florence. The south hosts nearly 20 per cent of these visitors.

Success has brought some problems. Many of the jobs in tourism are only seasonal. There is a lot of illegal, unplanned building along coastal areas. Unregulated construction around scenic landscapes such as the Bay of Naples, for example, has led to the imposition of more rigid planning controls.

Romans' holidays

Although more and more Italians travel abroad on holiday every year – spending over £10,000 million abroad in 1999 – 83% still choose to visit resorts in their own country. Italians have long holidays in comparison to other European countries – between four and six weeks a year, taken as longer trips of two weeks or more in summer and short breaks at other times of the year.

In August, some factories shut down for a month and many shops also close for the period, especially around 15 August, the Feast of the Assumption, which is called *Ferragosto*. Traditionally, this is the period when the Italian population heads for the beaches. Large cities such as Milan and Turin are less busy because so many residents have left to go to beach resorts. In the busiest summer season, a large resort such as Rimini on the Adriatic coast has up to 2 million visitors from Italy and other parts of Europe. Some coastal towns make 90% of their income during this one month. The fact that many Italians take their holiday at the same time can cause large traffic jams on the main roads, and seats on trains are hard to find. The *rientro* (literally, re-entrance), when Italians return to the cities, also causes major problems.

COMMUNICATIONS AND TRANSPORTATION

The telephone system in Italy is modern and fully automated. There are over 26 million telephones in the country. As in most of western Europe, mobile phones are also very popular.

The historic centres of many Italian cities are not very well adapted for large-scale traffic. People use small cars and motorbikes to get around. Workers and students also use trains to commute into larger towns and cities. People may also travel to work or school by bus or, in the major cities, by tram.

Road transportation

Italy's road network is extensive and efficient. The main roads extend for 305,388 kilometres (189,340 miles), most of which is paved. The excellent *autostrada* (motorway) system covers more than 6940 kilometres (4302 miles) and links all the main Italian cities. Car travellers pay expensive tolls to use the *autostrada*. The system was massively expanded during the period from 1955 to 1975, partly spurred on by the rapid increase in car ownership during this time. Italy's main roads were largely built by private companies employed by the government, and building has been funded by tolls. Freight is largely carried by road because of the slow expansion of the railway network during the 20th century. Car ownership in Italy is high and this has caused problems of pollution and congestion in the country's city centres. Some cities, such as Milan and Bologna,

MAIN FOREIGN ARRIVALS

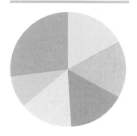

%

17 Switzerland

16 France

16 Germany

15 Yugoslavia

9 Austria

27 others

source: Government of Italy

Made in Italy

The Italian people have been famous for many inventions. The *pantelgrafo*, a forerunner of the fax machine, was invented by Giovanni Caselli in 1856. Composer Gioacchino Rossini even sent a musical score by *pantelgrafo*. In 1871, Antonio Meucci designed a telephone but he could not afford to renew the patent, so Alexander Graham Bell was able to patent his telephone in 1876. Nobel prize-winning physicist Guglielmo Marconi (1874–1937) sent the first radio signals across the Atlantic in 1901.

The world's first motorway was the *autostrada* between Milan and Varese, which was opened in 1924.

TRANSPORTATION

Italy's best communications lie around the industrialized centres of the northern cities. In the south, public works projects suffer from funds being siphoned off through local corruption. Major national roads include the *Autostrada del Sole*, the motorway that links Milan with Rome and the south. **Alpine** tunnels link northern Italy with the rest of Europe, and an efficiently maintained system of roads links the country's major centres.

— main roads
┼┼┼┼ railways
✈ major airports
— navigable rivers

During the fascist period, Mussolini was famous for making the railways function efficiently. Today, people say that Italian trains have not run on time since!

close to private motor vehicles when pollution exceeds a certain level. This has led to attempts to introduce cleaner fuels for both public and private vehicles.

Rail travel in Italy is inexpensive compared to that of most European countries. Most of the railway network, which extends for 19,503 kilometres (12,092 miles), is state owned and heavily subsidized. Although the network is extensive, Italian trains are famous for arriving late. One train often waits for another before departing and thus causes a string of delays. A trip from Milan to Rome takes about four hours, while Rome to Naples takes about an hour and 45 minutes.

Although water transportation has been important in Italy's history, there are few internal waterways in the country. The Po River is the country's only navigable internal waterway. Italy has many merchant ships. For transportation of goods around Italy by sea, the main ports are Genoa, Naples, Civitavecchia, Taranto, Augusta (Sicily) and Olbia (Sardinia). Trieste, Genoa and Taranto are major ports for international trade.

The national airline, Alitalia, flies to many international destinations; in addition, charter airlines run services between Italy and major European cities. There are major international airports at Rome, Fiumicino (Leonardo da Vinci), and Milan, Malpensa.

When Greece, Spain and Portugal joined the European Union in the late 1980s, Italy faced fierce competition for its Mediterranean agricultural products, such as olive oil and fruit.

First or second capital?

Rome may be Italy's political capital, but there is no doubt that the serious and hard-working northern city of Milan is in every way the country's industrial centre. The Romans claim that the *Milanesi* lack a sense of humour and work too hard, while the Lombardians retort that the success of their industry – producing 30% of the country's tax revenues – subsidizes the capital.

For centuries, Milan was considered the capital of Italy by its foreign rulers – Charlemagne came here to be crowned – and it still shares extensive links with northern Europe, both cultural, industrial and through its excellent transportation links. Situated at the centre of the Po Valley, Italy's industrial heartland, Milan is also the hub for a complex north Italian transportation network. It has the country's largest stock market and is the city where north European companies come to trade. In addition, it is the acknowledged centre of Europe's design industry, and it outstrips Paris in terms of earnings from fashion. Other major industries in the region include vehicle production, electrical appliances (particularly domestic appliances), engineering components and chemicals. Milan is also the centre of Italy's Internet industry, although most other media are centred in Rome, including the state companies of the RAI (see page 105).

The downside to Milan's economic miracle is the urban sprawl that surrounds the ancient city centre and the smog that often makes the air hard to breathe. Restrictions are sometimes imposed to limit the number of motor vehicles entering the city, and face masks are donned by the city's traffic police.

Arts and living

*'There is no end. There is no beginning.
There is only the infinite passion of life.'*

Italian film director Federico Fellini

Italy has one of the richest cultural heritages of any modern nation. Its position at the centre of the Roman empire and then as the home of the **Catholic** Church made it a centre of work for artists. This encouraged the development of many different art forms. Historically, the peninsula's competing **city-states** fought to outdo each other in the lavishness of their decoration as they did in the ferocity of their military campaigns. This history gave the region a concentration of artistic riches unequalled in the Western world. Visitors to Italy are often astounded by the sheer accumulation of history and cultural artefacts that are found in even the smallest towns.

This inheritance from the past lives on in much of Italian life. Many people still live in buildings that are hundreds of years old, and local customs persist at almost every level – in the language, cuisine and *modi di fare* (behaviour) of each region.

There have been attempts to break with the past – notably during the **fascist** period. Contemporary Italy is influenced by the industrial culture of its northern towns. The country's leadership in world design, fashion and engineering affects much of its modern cultural life, and throughout Italian daily life, there is a strong feeling for the visual arts. Today, Italy is fortunate to mix the best of its historic past with the hi-tech economy and liberal institutions of a modern European state.

Italy's cuisine is a mixture of food and styles from different regions. Food in the north is generally heavier, while that of the south is spicier and sweeter.

FACT FILE

● With one doctor for every 169 people, Italy has the highest doctor–patient ratio in the world.

● At the beginning of the 20th century, only 2% of Italians actually used Italian as their main spoken language. Dialects were not challenged until the new education programmes were started after 1945.

● In the 18th century, young French artists who won the *Prix de Rome* went to study in Rome at the French Academy. It was felt that the young artists should base their studies on Rome's antiquities and the paintings of the **Renaissance**.

93

THE ARTS

Italy is unique in the Western world in that its artistic past has almost continually influenced the works of the present. It is possible to trace a tradition of rational non-religious culture that stretched from classical times to the Renaissance – values that are still visible in contemporary Italian society.

Architecture

Italy is full of historic architecture, some of it in ruins, some perfectly preserved. Most Italian cities have historic centres, ringed by suburbs of modern apartment blocks.

Although great Roman temples were built of marble and stone, others were built of brick or concrete. Styles were inspired not only by the straight beams and columns of ancient Greek buildings but also by the construction techniques of the Etruscans, who used arches and vaults. The Romans discovered that it was quicker to build using small stones and rubble held together with concrete than to cut large stone blocks and fit them together. Concrete was made from lime and fine volcanic earth. Stone was often used as a facing material to cover the wall underneath. Columns were decorated at the top with carved capitals.

This 1st-century fresco (wall painting) from a Roman villa at Pompeii displays a fine command of perspective. The Romans were strongly influenced by earlier Greek techniques.

Roman styles were revived with Romanesque architecture in the 11th century. Churches had round, arched windows, with carvings on external walls. Later, as building techniques improved, **Gothic** churches were built higher with tall, slim windows. Inside the impression was of light and a feeling of movement upwards emphasized by slender columns and pointed arches. Perhaps the most famous example of Italian Gothic is Milan Cathedral.

During the Renaissance, architects looked to ancient Greece for inspiration. When designing the dome of the cathedral in Florence, Filippo Brunelleschi (1377–1446) made a structure with simple lines. Other well-known Renaissance architects were Donato Bramante (1444–1514), who built the *tempietto* (small church) in Rome that allegedly covered the site of St Peter's martyrdom, Leon Battista Alberti (1404–72), who wrote a famous treatise on perspective, and Andrea Palladio (1508–80), whose *Four Books of Architecture* had a major influence on European architecture for over 200 years.

Baroque was the style of the 17th and 18th centuries. It was very elaborate, with façades filled with curves, carvings and statues. During this time, Gian Lorenzo Bernini designed St Peter's Square in Rome (see page 39).

Italians also enjoy good modern design. Italian architecture and the arts generally fell into decline after the late 18th century because of repeated invasions by foreign powers. A revival of sorts occurred in architecture under the fascists in the 20th century, with important buildings including the station at Florence (1933–35) and the Casa del Fascio in Como (1932–36). More recently, working with Pier Luigi Nervi (1891–1979) as structural engineer, Gio Ponti (1891–1979) is well known for

Pier Luigi Nervi developed the use of ferro cemento, a mixture of steel mesh and cement, which enabled him to construct vast but solid structures, such as this Tourist Pavilion built near Milan in 1960.

the Pirelli Building in Milan. Nervi often used reinforced concrete in his designs, including stadiums for the 1960 Rome Olympics and San Francisco Cathedral in the USA. Perhaps the most famous contemporary Italian architect is Renzo Piano (born 1937), who is responsible for the Pompidou Centre in Paris (1972–76, with British architect Richard Rogers) and for Kansai Airport in Japan (1994).

Painting and sculpture

In the late Middle Ages, talented artists were busy all over Italy, creating artworks for rich noblemen, bishops and the pope. Much of this work was produced for the Church, and paintings usually showed scenes from the Christian religion or from ancient legend.

Their work was important in the developments in art. Giotto (1266–1337) broke away from the stiff lines of **Byzantine** and Gothic art. In the frescoes he painted in Assisi, Padua and Florence, the figures are softer and more natural.

Copies of Ghiberti's ground-breaking designs for the Florence baptistery doors still adorn the building, which stands opposite the cathedral in the centre of the city.

During the Renaissance (from the 1350s onwards), new techniques brought great changes to painting. Artists began to understand the use of perspective, which gave a feeling of depth to pictures. In sculpture, Lorenzo Ghiberti (1378–1455) inspired others with his bronze panels for the Gate of Paradise on the baptistery in Florence. Another sculptor, Donatello (1386–1466), modelled natural-looking statues, including a bronze of the biblical hero David and the largest bronze statue of a rider on a horse made since Roman times, called *Gattamelata*.

Fifteenth-century painters such as Masaccio (1401–28), Paolo Uccello (1397–1475), Piero della Francesca (1420–92) and Andrea Mantegna (1431–1506) carefully studied the structure and proportions of the human body so that they could make their paintings more realistic. They lived and worked in flourishing commercial centres such as Florence, Venice, Mantua, Arezzo and Perugia, travelling to other cities to complete commissions for clients.

In the following century, master painters such as Titian (1490–1576), Tintoretto (1518–94) and Veronese (1528–88) worked in Venice, creating artworks for the many churches in the city and for the head of the Venetian state, the **doge**. Raphael (1483–1520), who spent many years working for the pope in Rome, painted calm, balanced pictures. He was an excellent portrait painter and took care to perfect the details, even hands. Painting hands can be difficult, and some painters charged more for including them in portraits. Raphael used the hands to show more about the personality of the person he was painting.

Sandro Botticelli's masterpiece Primavera *(Spring) depicts various allegorical figures. From left to right they are: Mercury, messenger of the gods; the Three Graces; Venus, representing humanity; Flora, goddess of flowers and spring; the earth nymph Chloris and Zephyr, the west wind.*

Developments in painting

There were no art schools in medieval Italy. To learn about painting, boys became apprentices and worked in the artist's workshop. There was a lot to learn. Up until the 15th century, paintings were done on wood or on wet plaster (a technique known as fresco). The apprentices put a coat of fine plaster on the wall. An outline of the fresco was marked out with charcoal. Then the artist had to work quickly to finish the fresco before the plaster dried.

The paint colours – pigments mixed with eggyolk and water – sank into the wet plaster and merged with it. Once dry, the painting could not be changed.

In the late 1400s, artists started to work on canvas stretched over a wooden frame. It was easy to move and did not crack when the temperature changed. Artists found that adding linseed or walnut oil to colour pigments made a smooth, shiny paste. This oil paint dried slowly, allowing changes to be made.

Michelangelo's Pietà, *representing the Virgin Mary and the dead Christ, was sculpted when the artist was only 25 years old.*

Two of the world's great artists emerged in the 15th century: Leonardo da Vinci and Michelangelo. Both were good examples of Renaissance men – a term given to individuals who worked in more than one discipline and were talented in several different areas. The abundance of learning and culture during this period also encouraged people to explore new directions in artistic techniques and the sciences.

Leonardo (1452–1519) was not only a very talented artist but also a scientific genius. In his masterpieces, such as the *Last Supper* and the *Mona Lisa*, he created some of the most famous depictions of the human form. As a military engineer and architect, he designed many extraordinary machines, including what looked like an early version of a helicopter. His other interests included anatomy, botany, geology, hydraulics and mechanics. Although Leonardo had worked mainly in Milan, he died at the court of the French king, Francis I, for whom he was chief painter and architect from 1516.

Michelangelo Buonarotti (1475–1564) worked for the Medici family in Florence and then for the pope in Rome. He is famous for his expressive sculptures, especially his *David*. This statue, sculpted out of white marble, stands 4 metres (12 feet) high, twice human height. Michelangelo also spent years painting scenes from the Bible on the ceiling of the Sistine Chapel in the Vatican and wrote poetry. At the end of his life, he was chief architect on St Peter's in Rome.

The development of Michelangelo's painting and sculptural style into a freer line was a forerunner of the Baroque style of the 16th and 17th centuries, a fine example of which is the ceiling fresco of Sant' Ignazio in Rome. Two important artists of this period were Annibale Carracci (1560–1609) and Caravaggio (1571–1610). In sculpture, Gian Lorenzo Bernini (1589–1680) produced lavish and dramatic compositions for the churches of Rome. In the mid-18th century, Italian artists worked in the courts of France and Germany. Giovanni Battista Tiepolo (1696–1770) produced dramatic Baroque frescos, while Francesco Guardi (1712–93) and Canaletto (1697–1768) were chiefly patronized by foreign clients visiting their native Venice.

During the late 18th and early 19th centuries, Italian artists looked backwards to their illustrious past, and the incentives for creative art moved to France and northern Europe. From the late 19th century, the Italian *Divisionisti* depicted the play of light and shade on realistic subjects, often depicting workers or peasants in work

The Reformation and the emergence of Protestantism in northern Europe posed a real threat to the Catholic Church in Rome. As a result, the popes of the 16th century embarked on a Counter-Reformation and used the work of Renaissance artists to glorify Rome and the Catholic Church.

Artemesia Gentileschi

The Neapolitan Artemesia Gentileschi (1593–1652) was a rare example of a successful 17th-century woman painter. She portrayed realistic portraits and biblical scenes in rich colours, using deep shadow and dramatic perspective. The daughter of another successful painter, Orazio Gentileschi, she was influenced by Caravaggio's use of light and shade. She showed herself to be an astute businesswoman, carving a successful career in painting the Spanish nobles who ruled Naples at the time.

Giorgio di Chirico

Born in Vollos, Greece, in 1888 of Italian parents, de Chirico studied at the Academy of Fine Arts in Munich. His early work was linked with the Surrealist movement. The Surrealists placed emphasis on the imagination and the disturbing placement of unrelated objects and ideas. Di Chirico's paintings featured deserted, shadowy **piazzas**, rendered in flat colour and with unconventional elements, such as a banana and a marble bust. He moved to Paris in 1911 and was supported by Picasso and Guillaume Apollinaire. After 1919, his painting became more formal and academic and he disowned his earlier work (now considered his best). Later, he settled in Rome and worked intermittently until his death in 1978.

that echoed that of the French Impressionist painters. Perhaps foremost among the *Divisionisti* was Angelo Morbelli (1853–1919).

In the early 20th century, the most prominent Italian movement was that of Futurism. Launched in Milan in 1908 by the poet Emilio Marinetti (1876–1944), this movement marked a deliberate break with Italy's artistic past: 'Burn the museums! Drain the canals of Venice!' Marinetti declared. The movement took as its subject the depiction of speed and the new age of machines. Figures were often shown in movement. Futurist painting and sculpture frequently depicted events happening simultaneously. In the 1920s and 1930s, Futurism was revived under the dictatorship of Benito Mussolini.

In the 1960s, another important Italian movement was that of *Arte Povera* (Art of the Poor). Inspired by the ideals of equality popular during this period, the movement used 'found' or discarded materials to create sculptures and other artworks, and for the first time used modern materials such as plastics and objects of mass production.

Because Dante's *Divine Comedy* **was written in the Florentine dialect that later formed the basis of modern Italian, the work is often considered the first work of Italian literature. It has a similar importance in Italian to Shakespeare's work in English.**

Literature

Although as many as fourteen languages developed in Italy from Latin, until about 1200 it was not thought appropriate to write literature in these languages. Many poems were composed in Sicilian at the court of Frederic II. Saint Francis of Assisi (1182–1226) wrote his *Canticle of the Sun* in a local dialect, but Latin was still the proper language for educated people to write in. The Florentine poet Dante Alighieri (1265–1321) wrote a book explaining why he supported writing in local languages, but wrote it in Latin. Later, his long poem *The Divine Comedy* became the first major work of literature to be written in a local dialect. Dante wrote in the dialect derived from Latin that was spoken by the Florentines. This dialect later developed into what we know today as Italian.

The Divine Comedy has three sections: Hell, Purgatory and Paradise. Dante makes an imaginary journey through Hell, meeting people from Italy's past and friends and enemies. The journey is also about the progress of a soul towards God and human progress to peace on Earth.

The Renaissance provided a great flowering of literature in Italy as it did in the other arts. The most important writer of this period was Giovanni Boccaccio (1313–75), whose *Decameron*, a series of stories related by individuals escaping the plague in Florence, was a major influence on the English poet Geoffrey Chaucer.

Later, Alessandro Manzoni (1785–1873), who also came from Tuscany, was a leading writer of the Romantic period. His historical novel *The Betrothed* (1827) is very important because the way it was written became a model for modern Italian novels. The book is about how two poor peasants, Renzo and Lucia, marry despite the attempts of the local lord to stop them. Most Italians study this book in secondary school. Giovanni Verga (1840–1922) wrote about the people of Sicily. He described the life of farmworkers in a realistic way. Author Grazia Deledda (1871–1936) brought to life the people of

The Florentine writer Dante is shown outside the walls of his native town (the dome of the cathedral is visible on the right). To the left are the circles of Hell described in his Divine Comedy.

Sardinia. For her short stories and novels she was awarded the Nobel Prize for Literature in 1926. Italo Svevo (1861–1928) and Oscar Pirandello (1867–1936) brought the influences of psychology and Modernism to the Italian novel and drama at the beginning of the 20th century, while Ignazio Silone (1900–78) wrote about the harsh life of southern Italians and the need for reforms. Later Italian novelists of note include Italo Calvino (1923–85) and Umberto Eco (born 1932). The latter, a university professor from Bologna, achieved international fame with his first novel *Il Nome della Rosa* (*The Name of the Rose*), which was made into a film starring Sean Connery.

Opened in 1778, Milan's La Scala is one of the world's great opera houses. The first work performed here was by Antonio Salieri, portrayed in the film Amadeus as Mozart's great rival.

Music

The notation that we use for music was invented in Italy, and many of the terms that we use to describe the way a piece of music should be played – such as *allegro* (fast or happy), *fortissimo* (very loud) and *crescendo* (increasing in volume) – are taken from Italian. The country

also played a central role in the development of musical forms. The first musical score printed with movable type was created in Venice in the 16th century. Opera began in Florence at the end of the 16th century and spread to Venice, where the first opera theatre opened in 1637. Perhaps the most famous Italian composer from this period is Claudio Monteverdi (1567–1643), although his fame was soon superseded by that of the Venetian Antonio Vivaldi (1675–1741), whose *Four Seasons* is still much performed. However, it was in the 19th century that Italian composers dominated the modern opera with the light operas of Rossini (1792–1868) such as *The Barber of Seville* (1816) and *William Tell* (1829), Donizetti (1797–1848) and

Lucrezia Borgia (1833), Bellini (1801–35) and *Norma* (1831), Puccini (1858–1924) and *La Bohème* (1896), *Tosca* (1900) and *Madama Butterfly* (1904) and, above all, Giuseppe Verdi (1813–1901) and *La Traviata* (1853) and *Aïda* (1871). These works achieved an importance in the history of opera that has never been surpassed.

Born in Parma in northern Italy in 1935, the tenor Luciano Pavarotti has achieved international fame both with public performances and with a series of successful recordings.

The film industry

Although the Italian film industry produced some notable spectacular films in the silent era, by the early 1930s, Italian studios were approaching bankruptcy. The industry was placed under government control by Mussolini in the late 1930s and early 1940s, and a vast film complex called Cinecittà was built outside Rome by the fascists. In its first years, Cinecittà was tainted by its production of fascist propaganda films, works that became increasingly

The director Federico Fellini, who was born at Rimini in north-east Italy, stands in front of a poster for his most famous film, La Dolce Vita.

important with Italy's entrance into World War Two. Later, however, the studios became the centre of the Italian film industry. Postwar Italian film was dominated by a movement known as neo-realism, which took a direct and unsentimental look at Italian life. Perhaps most striking among the work of this period is Roberto Rossellini's (1906–77) *Roma Città Aperta* (*Rome Open City*, 1945) and *Germania Anno Zero* (*Germany Year Zero*, 1947), both of which show conditions in postwar Europe. Other major talents of neo-realism were Luchino Visconti (1906–76) and Vittorio De Sica. De Sica's 1948 *Ladri di Biciclette* (*Bicycle Thieves*) has become a classic of European cinema.

It was, however, in the 1960s that Italian film achieved its greatest success, with Cinecittà becoming known as the Hollywood of Europe. Rome itself became a centre of the international jet set as the economy boomed. The scene was portrayed by Federico Fellini (1920–94) in his *La Dolce Vita* (1960), the first of a series of very stylish films starring the actor Marcello Mastroianni (1924–96). Mastroianni was the first of a number of Italian actors, including Sophia Loren (born 1934) and Gina Lollobrigida (born 1927), to achieve truly international fame. Other notable directors of the 1960s were Pier Paolo Pasolini (1922–75) and Michelangelo Antonioni (born 1912). The 1970s saw the emergence of another major director in the figure of Bernardo Bertolucci (born 1941), whose *Last Tango in Paris* (1972) starred Marlon Brando. Bertolucci's *The Last Emperor* (1987), which depicted the life of the last emperor of China, won eight Academy Awards (Oscars). More recently, the sentimental *Cinema Paradiso* (1988), *Il Postino* (*The Postman*, 1994) and *La Vita è Bella* (*Life Is Beautiful*, 1997) have achieved international fame, the latter winning an Oscar for its director and star, Roberto Beningni (born 1952).

The media

There are three main state TV channels called the RAI. Traditionally, each of these has been associated with a specific political party. Cable and satellite stations are also numerous. The largest media conglomerate in Italy is Silvio Berlusconi's Finivest, which owns Canale 5.

Important national daily papers include *Corriere della Sera* (*Evening Courier*), *La Stampa* (*The Press*) and *La Repubblica* (*The Republic*). In addition to watching sports on TV, fans love to read about it. There are three newspapers and fifteen magazines dedicated to

Newspaper stands at main stations and town centres sell a variety of partworks (books split into several parts) as well as the usual magazines and newspapers.

sports reporting. The best-selling title, *Il Corriere dello Sport*, sells 573,000 copies a day, compared to a big circulation national paper like *Corriere della Sera*, which sells around 874,000 copies. The **Communist** Party's national newspaper, *L'Unità* (*Unity*), folded in the late 1990s.

DAILY LIFE

Life in Italy is usually centred around the family, and people often rely on family members to help them in difficult times. Most young people still live at home until they marry. Seventy per cent of men remain living at home with their parents until they are 35. Italian men have a reputation for liking to be spoiled by their mothers and having all their meals cooked and their washing done. This can cause problems later when they marry because their wives are not prepared to do all this work for their husbands, especially if they work themselves.

Getting married is still important in Italy, but fewer and fewer children are being born. In the 1960s, it was

Italian cafés serve a variety of coffees, light snacks and some alcoholic drinks. They charge extra for a seat, and many people drink standing up at the bar rather than pay the extra cost.

How to say ...

In general, Italian is written exactly as it is spoken and is an easy language for English speakers to learn. Double consonants indicate a longer sound.

Please	*Per favore* (PURR fav-OR-ay)	
Thank you	*Grazie* (GRAR-zee-ay)	
Yes	*Sì* (SEE)	
No	*No* (NOH)	
Hello	*Buongiorno* (BWON-JEE-OR-noh)	
Goodbye	*Arrivederci* (aree-ve-DER-chee)	
Good evening	*Buona sera* (BWONA-SER-ah)	
Good night	*Buona notte* (BWONA-NOT-ay	
How are you?	*Come stai?* (KOM-ay STY) (informal); *Come sta?* (KOM-ay-STA) (formal)	
I understand	*Ho capito* (OH-ka-PEE-toh)	
I don't understand	*Non ho capito* (NON-OH-ka-PEE-toh)	

Numbers

One	*Uno* (OO-no)	
Two	*Due* (DOO-ay)	
Three	*Tre* (TRAY)	
Four	*Quattro* (KWOT-roh)	
Five	*Cinque* (CHING-kway)	
Six	*Sei* (SAY)	
Seven	*Sette* (SETT-ay)	
Eight	*Otto* (OTT-oh)	
Nine	*Nove* (NOH-vay)	
Ten	*Dieci* (dee-YAY-chee)	

Days of the week

Sunday	*Domenica* (doh-MEN-icah)
Monday	*Lunedi* (LOON-edee)
Tuesday	*Martedi* (MAR-tedee)
Wednesday	*Mercoledi* (MER-cole-dee)
Thursday	*Giovedi* (JO-veh-dee)
Friday	*Venerdi* (VEN-er-dee)
Saturday	*Sabato* (SAB-at-oh)

common to find families with three or four children. Now Italy has the eighth-lowest birth rate in the world (behind Latvia, Bulgaria, Germany, Ukraine, Slovenia, Sweden and Austria), and most families have only one child. If the birth rate continues as it is at present, by 2050, the current Italian population of 57.6 million will have dropped to 41 million. Women are waiting longer to have children for career or economic reasons. Because of the close connection between the state and the Catholic Church, divorce became legal in Italy only in 1971 and Italy's divorce rate is among the lowest in the world.

EDUCATIONAL ATTENDANCE

college and university — 41%

secondary school — 88%

primary school — 98%

source: Government of Italy

All Italian men over eighteen years of age may be called up for military service in the army or air force for a year, or for eighteen months in the navy. Recruits also serve in the *carabinieri*, a type of local police force charged with keeping the peace and controlling minor offences.

Education

Italian children attend school between the ages of six and sixteen. The school year runs from September to the end of June. Pupils attend classes from 8 or 8:30 a.m. until around 1:30 or 2 p.m.

From the age of three to five, children often attend play school before they start school at age six. After five years at primary school, pupils go to secondary school at the age of eleven. *Scuola media* (middle school) lasts three years. The subjects that pupils study are Italian, history and civic education, geography, maths, science, a foreign language and art. For those who want to study further at college, there are another five years of study. Students can choose from arts-based or science-oriented courses at a *liceo* (college), specialized vocational instruction at technical schools or teacher training.

If pupils do not get good marks at the end of a school year, they are not allowed to go on to the next year. On average, 20.5 per cent of boys and 11.6 per cent of girls have to repeat a year.

All students who have a *maturità* (secondary school) diploma can attend a university. Undergraduate degree courses at university can last between four (for law or philosophy) and six years (for medicine). Some subjects are so popular that the number of students has been limited by entrance tests. Tuition fees are relatively low, but students do not receive grants for living expenses. Some Italian students study and work part-time and take a long time to finish their degrees.

Religion

Most Italians – 84 per cent – would call themselves Catholics. The Catholic Church and the **papacy** have had a huge influence on the cultural life of Italy, and social attitudes in the country have been shaped largely by the Church. Despite this, only one in three Italians goes to mass every Sunday. Fewer young people are volunteering to become priests or nuns. Only one-third of priests are under 50 years of age, and 44 per cent are between 50 and 60.

In many communities, the parish priest still has an important role. He gives parishioners spiritual comfort, but also has many contacts through the community that enable him to help with jobs or other practical matters.

Some people who are disappointed with traditional Catholic worship look for spiritual inspiration elsewhere. The second-largest religious group is **Protestant**, including the Lutherans of the German-speaking communities of the north-east. There is a small Muslim community in the south of Italy and in some cities of the north, mostly originating in the immigrant communities from northern Africa. In addition, Italy has a small Jewish population. Despite Italy's fascist past, the Jewish community has been treated much better by the ordinary Italian people than in many other parts of Europe.

Annual processions with effigies of saints are common in Italy. Here a figure of San Antonio di Padova is carried through the streets of Rome.

Celebrations

There are many religious festivals in Italy as well as other public holidays. If the holiday falls on a Tuesday or a Thursday, people usually take extra time off on Friday or Monday. They call the extended holiday *il ponte* (the bridge).

The Christmas holiday in Italy is two days – Christmas Day and St Stephen's Day on 26 December. Italians eat panettone, a light traditional cake with dried fruit, at

National holidays

1 January	New Year's Day
6 January	Epiphany
April	Easter Monday
25 April	Liberation Day
1 May	Labour Day
15 August	Feast of the Assumption
1 November	All Saints' Day
8 December	Feast of the Immaculate Conception
25 December	Christmas Day
26 December	St Stephen's Day

HOW ITALIANS SPEND THEIR MONEY

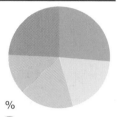

%

26.3 housing

19.4 food

17.3 transportation

6.7 clothing

6.0 leisure

24.3 other

source: Italian National Statistical Institute

During the first weekend of May, pilgrims in the southern town of Bari follow a boat out to sea carrying an image of San Nicola. The pilgrims then hold a ceremony out at sea. The pilgrimage is in honour of the 47 sailors who are believed to have saved the saint's life.

Christmas. The New Year holiday is 1 January. Epiphany (6 January) celebrates the arrival of the Three Kings and can be another time for giving gifts. Easter is celebrated on Easter Sunday and the following Monday is also a holiday. Assumption on 15 August honours the Virgin Mary and falls when most people are on holiday for the month of August.

All Saints' Day on 1 November is a sombre occasion when people remember family members or friends who have died. The Feast of the Immaculate Conception on 8 December celebrates the time when the Virgin Mary was told her child would be the Son of God.

Two non-religious public holidays come close together: Liberation Day on 25 April and Labour Day on 1 May. Liberation Day marks the surrender of the German and Italian fascist soldiers in World War Two.

In addition to these holidays, each Italian region has its own special festivals. Towns and villages honour their patron saint with processions and fireworks. Some celebrations go back many centuries. In Siena, a horse race called the Palio is held, named after the banner that the winning rider receives. It dates back to the Middle Ages and is held every 2 July and 16 August (see opposite).

At the beginning of Lent, the period before Easter, people celebrate carnival by dressing up in costumes and wearing masks. Easter is the most important Christian festival, and there are special Easter celebrations in many regions of Italy, especially in the south.

WHAT DO ITALIANS OWN?

27.9%	35.3%	20%	37%	62.3%	28%
microwave ovens	mobile telephones	computers	fax machines	video recorders	dishwashers

Source: Italian National Statistical Institute

Besides religious festivals, towns hold festivals to celebrate a kind of food or wine. It could be a harvest of cherries, chestnuts, fish or wine. If it is mushrooms, people try out dishes with mushrooms as a main ingredient.

Food

Italian food is one of the great cuisines of the world. Italians are very proud of their cooking and like to take care about what they prepare. Compared to many countries, there are few foreign restaurants in Italy. Italians even prefer home-grown fast food such as pizza or focaccia, a baked slice of pizza dough flavoured with olive oil and herbs or olives.

To start the day, Italians like a coffee. The basic cup of coffee is an espresso, a small cup of strong coffee made with freshly ground coffee beans. It is drunk with sugar but no milk. Breakfast may be a slice of bread and jam with an espresso, a cappucino or a caffèlatte (coffee with hot

The Palio

The Palio is a bareback horse race held in the Tuscan city of Siena twice each summer in honour of the Virgin Mary. Siena is split into seventeen different *contrade* (districts) and ten of these districts compete against each other at each Palio. The *palio* itself is a silk banner, which the winners display in their local headquarters after the race. During the competition, the riders tear around Siena's main square, the shell-shaped Piazza del Campo, on a track of packed dirt. A horse without a rider can still win the race and riders are frequently thrown off and injured. Horses are sometimes taken into the local churches for a blessing before the race.

Pizza

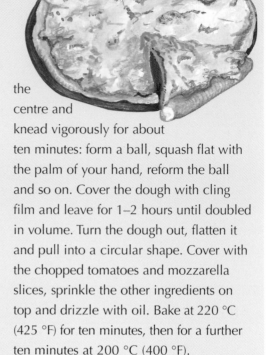

You will need:

1 tbsp of dry yeast

250 ml/ 9 fl oz warm water

350 g/12 oz plain flour plus more
   for kneading

salt

1 tin of chopped tomatoes

1 whole mozzarella, sliced

handful of basil leaves

10 pitted black olives

1 tbsp of extra virgin olive oil

Dissolve the yeast in the water. Make a mound of the flour and scoop out a bowl in the centre. Put the yeast mixture and salt in the bowl. Mix in a circular motion with a fork until a dough forms. Sprinkle a work surface with flour. Put the dough in the centre and knead vigorously for about ten minutes: form a ball, squash flat with the palm of your hand, reform the ball and so on. Cover the dough with cling film and leave for 1–2 hours until doubled in volume. Turn the dough out, flatten it and pull into a circular shape. Cover with the chopped tomatoes and mozzarella slices, sprinkle the other ingredients on top and drizzle with oil. Bake at 220 °C (425 °F) for ten minutes, then for a further ten minutes at 200 °C (400 °F).

milk). For lunch in big cities, workers eat in small restaurants like a trattoria, where the food is cooked fresh, or at a *tavola calda* (literally, 'hot table') with ready-cooked cold roast meat, grilled vegetables and salads of lettuce, rice or pasta. In smaller towns, people often go home for lunch.

A traditional Italian meal may include appetizers of salami and Parma ham or a salad. Next comes the first course of soup, risotto (a rice dish) or pasta, followed by the second course of meat or fish served with vegetables. To finish, there is cheese, then fruit or a dessert. People often have a glass of Italian wine to go with the food.

There are many regional dishes, depending on the climate and what grows in the area. In northern Italy, people use more butter than olive oil for cooking. Generally, the food in northern Italy is heavier, with more meat and dairy produce, rich cheeses and cream and stuffed egg pasta, such as ravioli. Rice is also grown in the north, so there are a lot of recipes for risotto. In the south, pasta is made from wheat alone, with no added eggs, and there is greater use of spices – reflecting southern Italy's history of trading with the east. People also eat less meat in the south.

Pasta was introduced from China by Marco Polo, but now people all over Italy eat it. There are more than 600 types, named for their shape. Spaghetti means 'little strings', *farfalle* are 'butterflies', *conchiglie* are 'shells' and *penne* are short, round tubes. Sauces for pasta are varied, too. Traditionally, spaghetti with tomato sauce comes from Naples, so the sauce is called *napoletana* in Italian. Pesto is associated with Liguria. It is made from basil and pine nuts, an important ingredient that is commonly found in the region.

About two-thirds of Italians live in cities or urban areas, although slightly more people in the south than in the north live in the country. Italians are more likely to buy their homes than to rent them, and families often help their children buy a home when they get married. The central areas of Italian cities are full of low-rise historic buildings, some of which may have

In northern Italy, Parmesan is used to flavour pasta dishes, but in the south, people use *pecorino*, a sharp-tasting sheep's cheese, to give the dish extra taste.

The majority of Italians today live in low-rise apartment blocks, such as these on the outskirts of the Tuscan town of Prato.

Out for a stroll

When they have time, many Italians like to take an evening stroll, called a *passeggiata* in Italian. Between 6 and 8 p.m., people stroll around the main square or streets of the town, sometimes stopping to chat with friends. Large groups of people can be seen enthusiastically discussing the latest news about family and friends, sports or politics, and often it can be quite noisy.

been divided into offices or apartments. The streets are often narrow because they were built before cars were invented. Some older city apartment buildings have a central courtyard with gardens and trees. Further out from the centre, people live in modern apartment blocks. An apartment block is often called a *palazzo*, the same word that is used for a 'palace'.

In the south, people who farmed the land used to live in towns and go out to work in the fields. Today, more people have built new homes on their land.

Far fewer people live in country areas than in the past, especially in more remote or mountain areas. Young people prefer to move away to the nearest town or to a large city to find work and a more lively lifestyle.

Sports

Many Italians can be very passionate about sports, especially football, cycling and car racing. As in the UK, professional football is a multimillion-pound business in Italy. Many players from other countries in Europe, Latin America and Africa come to Italy to play because they are paid high relocation fees and salaries. In the professional leagues, the best teams play in the *Serie A* (A Series). *Serie-A* teams aim to win the *scudetto*, the shield given to the team that wins the most points during the season. Big cities often have two rival teams: Milan has AC Milan and Inter, Turin has Juventus and Torino and Rome has Lazio and Roma. Fans identify very strongly with their home teams, and the star footballers playing for their side are idolized by their fans.

Italian teams are also very successful internationally. The national team is known as *gli azzurri* (the blues) because they play in bright blue shirts. Italy has won the World Cup three times, in 1934, 1938 and 1982.

Volleyball is very popular in Italy and is often played on the beaches in summer. Italy's national team has won the world championship seven times and regional teams often win international competitions.

Cycling is popular with many Italians. Amateur cyclists can be seen out on the roads on weekends. The main Italian road race is the *Giro d'Italia*. Starting in late May or early June, it lasts three weeks and goes all over the peninsula.

Italy has a great tradition in international car racing, with two Formula 1 circuits. One is at Monza, north of Milan, where the Italian Grand Prix is held, and the other is the San Marino Grand Prix, held on the track at Imola in Emilia-Romagna. Ferrari is a top designer and manufacturer of racing cars.

Other sports that are popular are traditional ones, such as bowls, and basketball and volleyball. Italian competitors have also performed well internationally in yachting events and rowing.

Formula 1 racing cars enter the pit lane at the Imola Grand Prix in central Italy.

The future

'It [the European Union] will be a deterrent to the darker forces within Italian society.'

Antonio di Pietro, head magistrate in the *Tangentopoli* scandal

Italy today is a thriving **democratic** country with a rich past and a dynamic future. In spite of this, there are some enduring problems, including the economic differences between the north and the south, organized crime and inefficient public administration.

Into Europe

The European connection is seen by many Italians as something that is very important for the future. In opinion surveys, many people say that they think that being in the **European Union** (EU) will bring more efficient public administration, better economic growth and more jobs. They also feel that the use of one currency, the euro, by all the member countries of the EU will make Italy more competitive and give it more outlets to trade its goods.

Italians believe that being part of the EU will force the government to be more disciplined in running the country's finances because it has to meet targets set by supranational institutions (those operating across several different nations). Even now, there is still a large unofficial, or 'black', economy – illegal smuggling and trading of goods – which is estimated to be around 20 per cent of Italy's entire gross national product (GNP). The government is trying hard to bring this sector into the official system so it can raise taxes from its income.

The clear waters of Lake Como's picturesque shoreline have recently been the subject of extensive legislation to protect their purity.

In the EU, individual regions as well as countries feel they have a place and are given financial help from a central fund to which all members contribute. This may help Italy with its north–south divide. It may also limit the power of political groups such as the *Lega Nord* (Northern League), which wants northern Italy to become a separate state so that the north no longer has to contribute to supporting the south (see page 75).

A falling birth rate means that Italy may soon have a population closer in size to that of Spain than to those of France or the United Kingdom, whose size it resembles today.

An ageing population

At the moment, official statistics record more deaths than births in Italy. The average number of children needed per family to keep the population stable is 2.05. Italy's average number of children per family is only 1.2. This means that the population is getting older, without enough people being born to take on jobs and make enough money later to support the older citizens. Almost one in five Italians is over the age of 65 and people are usually living longer.

State pensions are generous, and government employees used to be allowed to retire after working for 25 years. Now the system has been changed, and people have to contribute for 35 years or be at least 57 years of age before they can retire. The usual retirement age is 65 for men and 60 for women. Italy spends much more public money on paying for pensions than it does on children. About 10 per cent of the GNP goes to pay for pensions, while 5 per cent is spent on education.

One part of the population that is increasing is immigrants from north Africa and eastern Europe (the main countries are Morocco, the countries of the former Yugoslavia – Croatia, Bosnia-Herzegovina, Serbia, and Slovenia, and Macedonia – Albania, the Philippines and the USA). There are about 1 million official immigrants, but there are also perhaps between 1 and 2 million illegal immigrants. Large groups come from Morocco and Albania, which have languages, religions and cultures that are very distinct from those of their host country.

In Italy – where people are highly aware of even regional differences – Italians are learning to see themselves as part of a multicultural society. There has recently been discussion about allowing immigrants to build mosques in Italy – a matter of some contention because the Catholic Church has been prevented from building churches in some Muslim countries.

The environment

Fighting pollution poses many problems for Italy today. The huge amount of air pollution generated by cars in cities causes damage to ancient monuments and historic buildings. Bologna and some other cities have banned private cars in some areas. Florence is experimenting with buses that use a mixture of gas and electricity in the historic city centre, while the smaller city of Ravenna in north-eastern Italy uses buses that run on methane.

In some lakes and sections of the northern Adriatic, the discharge of too many fertilizers and detergents led to too much algae being produced. This is especially a problem in the Po Valley, the country's main industrial and agricultural region. Waters flow from the fields of the surrounding farmland, bringing with them large amounts of fertilizers, and these mix with industrial waste to make the Po River the most polluted in the country. Where the Po flows into the sea, near Ravenna in the northern Adriatic, great masses of algae appear in the water all along the coast. The effect of this problem on Italy's tourist industry and pressure from environmental groups have led to attempts to clean up the area.

Hunters are a powerful lobby group, and in 1990 they won a referendum on whether hunting should be banned. Attempts have been made to limit the hunting season but many species, particularly small songbirds, are still at risk.

119

Almanac

POLITICAL

country name:
official long form: Italian Republic
short form: Italy
local long form: *Repubblica Italiana*
local short form: *Italia*

nationality:
noun: Italian(s)
adjective: Italian

official language: Italian

capital city: Rome

type of government: republic

suffrage (voting rights): everyone
eighteen years and over

national anthem: '*Fratelli d'Italia*'
('Brothers and Sisters of Italy')

national holiday: 25 April
(Liberation Day)

flag:

GEOGRAPHICAL

location: southern Europe; latitudes
39° to 47° north and longitudes
7° to 18° east

climate: Alpine in the north;
Mediterranean in the centre
and south

total area: 301,268 sq km
(116,293 sq miles)
land: 98%
water: 2%

coastline: 7600 km (4723 miles)

terrain: mostly mountainous, some
plains, coastal lowlands

highest point: Dufourspitze,
4634 m (15,203 ft)

lowest point: sea level

natural resources: mercury, potash,
marble, sulphur, coal, natural
gas, oil

land use:
arable land: 37.9%
forests and woodland: 23%
permanent pastures: 15%

permanent crops: 10%

other: 14.1%

POPULATION

population: 57.6 million

population density: 195 people per
sq km (504 per sq mile)

population growth rate (2000 est.):
0.09% (due to immigration)

birth rate (2000): 8.5 births
per 1000 of the population

death rate (2000): 10.9 deaths
per 1000 of the population

sex ratio (2000): 94.3 males per
100 females

total fertility rate (2000): 1.2 children
born per woman in
the population

infant mortality rate (2000):
5.4 deaths per 1000 live births

life expectancy at birth (2000):
total population: 78.7 years
male: 75.5 years
female: 81.9 years

literacy:
total population: 98.3%

ECONOMY

currency: euro (€);
€1 = 100 cents

exchange rate (2002):
£1 = €1.6

gross national product (2000):
£731,875 million (sixth-largest
economy in the world)

average annual growth rate
(1990–99): 1.4%

GNP per capita (2000): £12,694

average annual inflation rate
(1990–2000): 3.7%

unemployment rate (2000): 11.4%

exports (2000): £143,562 million
imports (2000): £134,937 million

foreign aid given (2000): £1131 million

Human Development Index
(an index scaled from 0 to 100 combining statistics
indicating adult literacy, years of schooling, life
expectancy and income levels):

90.3 (UK 91.8)

TIMELINE – ITALY

World history

Italian history

50,000 BC

*c.***40,000** Modern humans – *Homo sapiens sapiens* – emerge

*c.***4000 BC**
First permanent settlements in Italy

1500 BC

*c.***1200 BC** Italic and Ligurian tribes settle in northern and central Italy

8TH CENTURY BC
Greeks found colonies in southern Italy

*c.***1100 BC**
Phoenicians develop the first alphabetic script

*c.***612 BC** Fall of the Assyrian empire

*c.***563 BC** Birth of Siddharta Gautama, the Buddha

753 BC Founding of Rome

7TH–6TH CENTURIES
Peak of Etruscan culture in central Italy

400 BC

396 BC Romans defeat Etruscans

264–146 BC
Romans defeat Carthaginians in Punic Wars

327 BC
Alexander the Great reaches India

1259 Hanseatic League formed by merchants in Germany

1206 Delhi Sultanate set up in India

1096 First Crusade to reclaim Jerusalem begins

*c.***1000** Vikings reach American continent but do not settle

*c.***570** Birth of Mohammed in Mecca

*c.***AD 1** Birth of Christ in Roman province of Judea

30 BC Death of Cleopatra, last of the Ptolemies, in Egypt

1300 onwards
Rise of city-states in northern and central Italy

1282 War of Sicilian Vespers leads to Spanish intervention in southern Italy

1204 Fall of Constantinople to Venice

1000

AD 800
Charlemagne is crowned Holy Roman emperor in Rome

AD 560 Lombards invade Italy

AD 476 Fall of the Roman empire

AD 313 Emperor Constantine officially recognizes Christianity

AD 117 Under the Emperor Trajan, Rome reaches its greatest extent

27 BC Augustus becomes the first Roman emperor

44 BC
Assassination of Julius Caesar

50 BC

c.1350

1453 Constantinople falls to the Turks

1492 Columbus lands in America

1642–51 The English Civil War

c.1750 Industrial Revolution begins in England

c.1350–1550 Renaissance leads to rebirth of the arts and classical learning in Europe

1527 Sack of Rome by Holy Roman emperor, Charles V

c.1540 Counter-Reformation aims to re-establish dominance of Catholicism in Europe

1707 Conquest of Naples begins period of Austrian domination

2000 The West celebrates the Millennium – 2000 years since the birth of Christ

1989 Fall of communism in eastern Europe

2002 Italy adopts the euro as its national currency, replacing the lira

1996 Victory of Olive Tree Alliance, the first Italian government to include the former communists

1992 *Tangentopoli* scandal leads to downfall of a generation of politicians

1973–80 *Anni di Piombo*, period of terrorism in Italy

1969–71 *Autumno Caldo*, period of strikes and protests

1979 Former Soviet Union invades Afghanistan

1973 World oil crisis

1969 First man lands on Moon

1800

1789 French Revolution begins

1804 Napoleon becomes emperor of France

1815 Napoleon is defeated at Waterloo

1848 Famine prompts unrest and revolutions throughout Europe

1914–18 World War One

1797 Napoleon invades northern Italy

1861 Unification of Italy

1911 Italian invasion of Libya

1915 Italy declares war on Austria-Hungary and Germany

1922 Fascists march on Rome

1950

1945 World War Two ends, defeat of Germany

1941–45 Holocaust of European Jews

1939 World War Two begins.

1929 Wall Street Crash, beginning of the Great Depression

1946 Italy becomes a republic

1943 Mussolini arrested. Italy joins side of the Allies.

1939 Italy enters the war on the side of Japan and Germany

1936 Italy invades Abyssinia

Glossary

Abbreviation: Ital. = Italian

Alpine of the Alps mountains in northern Italy

Baroque style of art and architecture originating in Italy in the 16th century and characterized by extravagant contrasts of light and shade and elaborate decoration

Byzantine style of art and architecture from ancient Byzantium (now Istanbul), which emerged in the 4th century AD. Byzantine art mixed late Roman styles with early Christian symbolism and themes.

capitalism economic system based on supply and demand and private ownership of businesses and industry

cathedral large and important church

Chamber of Deputies lower house of the Italian parliament

city-state city that is an independent country with no allegiance to any larger region

comune (**Ital.**) standard administrative district in Italy; also the name of the local town hall

communism social and political system based on a planned economy in which goods and land are owned by everyone and in which there is no private property

democracy country where the people choose their government by election and where they hold supreme power

doge head of state in the historical Venetian republic

European Union (EU) organization made up of European countries that work together on many economic, social and political issues

fascist pertaining to the Fascist Party of Benito Mussolini, which came to power in 1922 in Italy and adopted an authoritarian, repressive regime based on a planned economy

Gothic style of art and architecture originating in Italy in the 12th century. Largely religious in subject matter, characterized by formal depictions of the human figure and (in architecture) by soaring, intricately carved stone structures, it became the accepted style for Christian art in western Europe for several hundred years.

left wing describes political ideas, parties or individuals who support a social system based on equality of wealth and opportunity and a more liberal social programme; also supportive of more government control in business and social legislation

lira Italian currency before it was replaced by the euro in 2002

mafia criminal organization operating in southern Italy with historical links to the feudal system of the region

mafioso (**Ital.**) (plural, *mafiosi*) member of the mafia

mezzogiorno (**Ital.**) (literally, 'midday') southern Italy

nationalism intense belief in importance of one nation's interests

open market market without tariffs (a charge imposed by government to limit certain types of trade) or other trade barriers

palazzo (**Ital.**) either a palace or an apartment block

papacy office of the pope in Rome

Papal States region of Italy controlled by the Church between the fall of the Roman empire and the establishment of the Italian republic

PDS (Ital.) acronym for the *Partito Democratico della Sinistra* (Democratic Party of the Left), the former Italian Communist Party and currently the largest left-wing party in the country

piazza large open square

pietà (**Ital.**) (literally, 'pity') sculpture or painting depicting the Virgin Mary supporting the dead Christ

Protestant member of the branch of Christianity that developed from the Reformation and the ideas of

Martin Luther. Separate from the Roman Catholic Church and the authority of the pope

Renaissance great revival of the arts and learning in Europe during the 14th to 16th centuries that built on a rediscovery of the arts of ancient Greece and Rome

republic government in which the citizens of a country hold supreme power and where all citizens are equal under the law

right wing describes political ideas, parties or individuals who support a more conservative approach to social matters and generally a less regulated approach to business

Risorgimento (Ital.) 19th-century Italian movement for independence from foreign rule

Roman Catholic member of the branch of Christianity based in Rome whose spiritual leader is the pope

Senate upper house of the Italian parliament. Formerly, the legislative assembly of the Roman empire

socialism social system involving the public ownership of goods and land. Less extreme than communism, it usually requires an element of democratic decision-making, rather than policy being imposed by the government or a small group of individuals.

Tangentopoli (Ital. 'Bribesville') Italian corruption scandal of the early 1990s, initially centred on Milan

Vatican centre of the Catholic Church in Rome and home of the pope

Bibliography

Major sources used for this book
Ginsborg, Paul, *History of Contemporary Italy* (Penguin, 1990)
Procacci, Guiliano, *History of the Italian People* (HarperCollins, 1987)
Richards, Charles, *The New Italians* (Penguin, 1992)
The Economist Pocket World in Figures (Profile Books, 2002)
Encyclopedia Britannica

General further reading
Bennett, Lynda A. (ed.) *Encyclopedia of World Cultures* (G. K. Hall & Co., 1992)
World Reference Atlas (Dorling Kindersley, 2000)
The Kingfisher History Encyclopedia (Kingfisher, 1999)
Student Atlas (Dorling Kindersley, 1998)
The World Book Encyclopedia (Scott Fetzer Company, 1999)

Further reading about Italy
Barzini, Luigi, *The Italians* (Penguin, 1964)
Hibbert, Christopher, *Rome: Biography of a City* (Penguin, 1985)
Lcvi, Carlo, *Christ Stopped at Eboli* (Penguin, 1982)
Vasari, Giorgio, *Lives of the Artists* (Penguin, 1965)

Some websites about Italy
Italy on the web
www.italyontheweb.org
Italian State Tourist Board
www.enit.it/default.asp?Lang=UK
The Italian Embassy in London
www.embitaly.org.uk

Index

Page numbers in *italics* refer to pictures or their captions.

Acknowledgements

Cover photo credit
Corbis: Vittoriano Rastelli

Photo credits
AKG London: 48, 53, 67, 71 **AKG Berlin:** S.Domingie 62, 96 British Library 63, Erich Lessing 51, 54, 94, 97, 101 **Corbis:** 102, Roger Antrobus 6, Araldo de Luca 98, Archivio Iconografico, SA 57, Jonathan Blair 24, 88 John Heseltine 37, L. Amos James 42, Robert Landau 18, Maurizio Lanini 32, David Lees 29, 95, 103, 104, Massimo Listri 61, Frank Owen 1, 40, Vittoriano Rastelli 84, 106, 115, Galen Rowell 21, Kevin Schafer 19, David Turnley 118, **Fiat:** 86, **Hulton Getty:** 73, **Hutchison:** John Egan 23, Robert Aberman 105, J. Davey 113, Robert Francis 78, Trevor Page 109, **Peter Newark's Pictures:** 64, **Robert Hunt Library:** 70, 72, **Stone:** Doug Armand 17, Joe Cornish 12, 33, 35, Robert Everts 117, Louis Grandadam 39, Nick Gunderson 22, Simon Huber 46, 111, Manfred Mehlig 16, Simon Watson 43, Randy Wells 26, Chris Windsor 92